**AHEAD O.**

AHEAD OF THE CURVE

Copyright © 2024 by Michael Harrison

All rights reserved.

No part of this publication may be reproduced, distributed, or transmitted in any form or by any means, including photocopying, recording, or other electronic or mechanical methods, without the prior written permission of the publisher, except as permitted by U.S. copyright law.

The story, all names, characters, and incidents portrayed in this production are fictitious. No identification with actual persons (living or deceased), places, buildings, and products is intended or should be inferred.

1st edition 2024

# CHAPTER 1

Felix Martin sat alone in his cramped second-story apartment, scouring the internet for anything that would give him a leg up on tomorrow's horse races. He was already into his bookie for fifteen grand, and he'd been dodging the guy for a week. But he believed his system would work this time. It had to. The bets just needed to be a little larger than usual.

There was a knock at the door, and Martin looked up from the screen of his laptop computer. When he cracked the door, two men in black jeans and matching black cowboy boots pushed through the opening and stormed into the apartment. One man wore a black button-down shirt, the other a skin-tight white tank top. The man in the tank top threw a devastating right hook to Martin's side, and he doubled over and collapsed to the floor.

"We've purchased your debt, Mr. Martin." The man in the button-down scowled, towering over the still wheezing Martin. "I expect fifty thousand dollars by the end of the week."

Martin looked up quizzically and attempted to stand. He

was quickly met with a sharp slap across his cheek, a blow that sent him down again.

"Please, please," he stammered. "I only owe fifteen. I can probably have five by the end of the week."

Another vicious slap, this time to the side of his head, sent Martin sprawling across the thread-bare carpet. Pain shot through his skull and a string of spit flew from his mouth as he fought to remain conscious.

As Martin struggled to gather himself, the man in the button-down bent over and whispered inches from Martin's ear, his breath an acrid blend of stale cigarette smoke and greasy fast food: "I said fifty thousand dollars by the end of the week. If I don't get my money, this will feel like a walk in the park."

When the men left, Martin lay motionless, less because of his injuries than utter despair. He had no way to get fifty grand—not by the end of the week or even by the end of the year. He was terrified—he had to run and hide. But how? Where? He'd been fired from his job. Lost his house. Sold his car. Now the only thing of value he had was a diploma from MIT and a vast knowledge of pharmaceutical chemistry that no one cared about because of his shoddy employment history.

Resigned to his fate, Martin didn't run. He didn't hide. Simply sat in his dingy, one-bedroom apartment and waited for the men to return.

As promised, they returned at the end of the week.

Martin, now resigned to torture, death or who knew what else, opened the door slowly to accept his fate.

The same two men barged in again, as they had before.

"Do you have my money?" Button-down said.

Martin replied with a blank stare and a shake of his head, then closed his eyes and lowered his head, waiting for the impending strike.

But none came. Martin slowly opened his eyes, unsure and uneasy, then hesitantly looked up.

"Didn't think so." A low chuckle from tank-top bounced around the room as button-down continued. "See Mr. Martin, I own you now. You work for me until the debt is paid."

Martin looked back at the man, eyes questioning. "Wha- what do you mean?" His voice trembled.

The man looked at Martin, a malicious smile across his face. "Let me show you."

---

Dillon Reynolds had been in a slump as of late, which is to say he wasn't even playing up to the mediocre standards expected of an average player on a small independent league club.

"Haaaa!" the umpire called, when a fastball slid over the middle of the plate.

Strike.

The next pitch came in high and fast. Reynolds took a mighty cut, grunting as he flung the barrel of the bat at the ball, hitting nothing but air.

Strike two. Not even close.

He thought he heard the catcher laugh under his breath, but didn't want to look back and give him the satisfaction.

"C'mon, man, focus," Reynolds muttered through clenched teeth.

He gathered himself. Took a deep breath and eyed the pitcher, guessing he would deliver something outside the strike zone. Probably get him to chase a bad pitch.

It was a poor guess. Another fastball grazed the plate low and away, and the umpire gave an emphatic punch-out signal.

Strike three.

Another 0-4 performance, and two more strikeouts to add to an ever-growing tally.

During the slow, painful walk back to the dugout, Reynolds wondered just how he had gotten to this valley—no, this *chasm*—in his career.

He'd always been the best player on every team he'd been a part of—hitting, pitching, fielding. A real five tool player. His senior year in high school, he'd measured six foot four inches tall, and tipped the scales at an even two hundred pounds.

He had the look of a ballplayer, too. Strong jaw line, a magnificent sandy blonde mullet, deep-set eyes that held a hint of mischief and that trademark Dillon Reynolds smile. The one he flashed after every home run. The girls loved that smile. He was never alone in the halls between classes, and there was never a shortage of fawning young ladies at his games.

Reynolds had been offered multiple collegiate scholarships out of high school but was also drafted in the second round, 48th overall, by the Arizona Diamondbacks in that year's Major League Draft. Eventually, thanks to a substantial signing bonus, Reynolds chose to forgo college and jump straight to the pros.

At eighteen years old, he was assigned to a Single-A club in California—the Visalia Rawhide. In Visalia, Reynolds' career took off like a moon shot leaving his bat. He tore through Low-A pitching and through 46 games tallied 19 home runs and a blistering .353 batting average.

Those kinds of numbers get noticed, and it wasn't long before he got a mid-season call up to the High-A club in Hillsboro, Oregon. The league was different: the results were the same. Homeruns, RBIs, singles, doubles—the stats piled up like sunflower seeds on the dugout floor after an extra inning game.

The following year, after Reynolds' torrid rookie season, he was assigned to the Diamondbacks' Double-A affiliate, the Amarillo Sod Poodles. In Amarillo, much as they had at his prior stops, his numbers jumped off the stat sheet. Reynolds had already garnered plenty of attention among the organization, but now the national media had started following the young star in waiting.

As had the fans. Everywhere he went, someone thrust a ball and a pen in his face, asking for an autograph or a selfie.

Arizona knew they had something special on their hands and wanted to see what Reynolds could do against some real Major League pitching. So, without as much as a cup of coffee in Triple-A ball, the big club gave Reynolds a September call up. The Diamondbacks were 27 games out of the playoffs, so there wasn't much to lose by giving playing time to a high-upside rookie. With a decent performance, they figured he might help sell some tickets for next season.

Not only were they right—they looked like geniuses. Through 14 games in the majors Reynolds' batting average registered a searing-hot .423 with 6 home runs, after each of which, he flashed that trademark smile. It was widely regarded as one of the best September performances in Major League history.

The national media fawned over Reynolds. He became an overnight media darling, with post-game interviews, television appearances, even an offer to be on one of the late-night talk shows. The sky was the limit.

Until it wasn't.

Armed with his recent success Reynolds went into the next spring training with great excitement and optimism. Over the first two weeks, he picked up right where he'd left off, battering the Arizona Cactus League pitchers one by one.

The last Saturday of Spring Training featured a doubleheader against Seattle. Reynolds was penciled in as the cleanup hitter in the second half of the back-to-back—a late afternoon game. His first at bat resulted in a seeing eye single and a run scored. A good start.

His next at bat came in the third inning. The late afternoon start meant the sun beat low in the Arizona sky, the glare obscuring the ball as it came out of the pitcher's hand.

The first pitch was a curveball that bounced in the dirt. Ball one.

The second pitch was a fastball that missed low and away. Ball two.

Reynolds was salivating now. Two balls, no strikes.

The third pitch was a fastball. High, but over the plate—just the way he liked it. Reynolds swung, heard the sweetly familiar *crack*, then flipped his bat, flashed his trademark smile at the pitcher and began the slow trot around the bases.

Until the umpire yelled: "Foul ball!"

Reynolds' head jerked toward the voice. He could have sworn the ball was fair. He must have been a hair early on his swing and pulled the pitch just outside left field foul pole.

The pitcher glared at Reynolds as he picked up his bat and ambled back into the batter's box, kicking at the red dirt as he walked.

The pitcher was a big guy from Venezuela—Jose Perez. Six foot four with a large round belly and a heater in the high nineties. Perez was a ten-year journeyman in the league and didn't appreciate being shown up by a cocky young kid like Reynolds.

Perez decided it was time the young slugger learned a

lesson in humility. He wound up and fired a fastball high and inside—a pitch designed to send a message. He'd thrown the same pitch many times before. The hitter would duck to prevent getting hit by the pitch or turn his back, letting it plunk him between the shoulders. There would be angry words and gestures and then the game would go on—the batter would get the point.

Perez wound up and, grunting with effort, heaved a heavy fastball towards Reynolds. Then, just at the point of release, he felt the ball slip—ever so slightly.

It was a perfect storm. Between the sun obscuring his vision and the ill-aimed fastball, Reynolds didn't have time to turn away from the pitch. The ball smashed into the side of his face at a speed of ninety-six miles per hour, shattering Reynolds' cheekbone.

The ball opened a massive gash under his left eye and blood began pouring from the wound.

Medical staff from both teams rushed onto the field and an ambulance was summoned as they attended to the downed slugger.

When the dust had settled, and the damage assessed, it was determined Reynolds had a fractured orbital socket and a globe rupture of his eye. The force of the ball impacting Reynolds' face had essentially caused his eyeball to burst. The result was a devastating loss of vision in his left eye.

The ophthalmologist had told him to stay positive. She'd said his vision could improve with time. And with each follow-up visit he hung on to that hope. He would strain at the eye chart, trying to force his vision to improve through sheer will, but the improvements were modest at best.

Mid-September that year, Reynolds was finally cleared to play again. He wasn't sure how the degraded vision would affect his game, but he was determined to get back on the field. He'd been training every day. Hitting off a tee. Fielding ground balls. Taking batting practice. But he knew there was no substitute for live game action.

The Diamondbacks—again multiple games out of a playoff spot—put Reynolds in the lineup right away to test their newly healed slugger.

The first game back was rough: 0-4 with three strikeouts, and a weak pop fly to the shortstop.

*I just need some time to adjust to live game speed,* he thought.

His teammates and coaches echoed his sentiments, which gave him comfort, but he was nagged by a feeling that something wasn't right.

The next game was a virtual carbon copy of the first. 0-4 with two strikeouts and a couple of middling grounders.

The poor performances came in succession, one after another. Over the handful of remaining games that season, Reynolds never even reached the Mendoza line. His .187 batting average was pitiful by major league, minor league, or even little league standards.

During the off season, the nagging in his head became a roar. But instead of accepting the fact that his vision would likely never return to normal, Reynolds began to rage against it. He worked tirelessly over the off season, racking up thousands of swings in the cage and countless hours in the gym.

But no matter how much work he put in, he couldn't force his swing back to form. It seemed his timing was perpetually off now. He was constantly behind the fastball and ahead of the curve. He couldn't identify pitches until it was too late.

Nothing was working.

As the winter progressed, so did Reynolds' anxiety about the upcoming season. Baseball used to be easy—a child's game he'd taken for granted. Now it seemed like one of those torturous desk jobs he'd always dreaded. The batting cage became a cubicle, and he was trapped in it until five o'clock, when he was mercifully released from his prison.

Much to his chagrin, the organization refused to give up on the crown jewel of their farm system. After the blistering September in his rookie season, they hoped last year was a fluke—a simple case of needing more at bats after a significant injury.

So the following season, despite batting a meager .225 in twenty Spring Training games, Reynolds made the opening day roster.

He started the season as the everyday first baseman and the cleanup hitter, a move designed by the coaching staff to buoy his confidence. After a string of poor performances at the plate, however, Reynolds was relegated to the bench where, between the occasional pinch-hit, he rode the pine and grappled with his thoughts.

It was mid-July when the call came. Art Moore, first year manager of a club that hadn't made the playoffs in seven years, called Reynolds into his office.

"Dillon," said Moore. "I'm going to cut to the chase. The organization thinks you'd benefit from some time in the minors."

Reynolds stared back. He'd never been demoted in his life and frankly he didn't know quite how to react. His voice failed him, and all he could manage was a long, slow sigh.

"I know that's not what you wanted to hear, but I'm not alone when I tell you I think that's what's best for your career right now." Moore sat back in his chair. "Get a few at bats, get your head right and you'll be back up in no time."

Reynolds stepped forward. "Look, Art, I know I've been struggling at the plate, but I feel like going to Triple-A is taking a step in the wrong direction." Reynolds replied, feigning surprise.

Moore cleared his throat. "You're not going to Triple-A. You're going back to Amarillo."

Now the surprise was genuine. In his head, Reynolds screamed a silent protest.

"Double-A?" he finally replied. "You know I don't belong in Amarillo Art."

The manager exhaled and absentmindedly shuffled a stack of papers on his desk. "It's an organizational decision. You need to get back to basics. Rebuild your foundation. Plus, you know the Amarillo club and some familiar faces might help you get back into form."

Reynolds shook his head. He didn't know if it was disgust, embarrassment, or anger. In any case, it was a feeling he didn't quite know how to process.

"Well coach," he muttered. "I'm sorry I let the team down."

---

Danny Rincon shook his head. He knew Diego couldn't hit the curveball and the catcher, his best friend Isaac, was calling for a fastball. This time Isaac put down three fingers.

*There's the curve*, Danny thought, then nodded and started into his windup.

The field was a deep, rectangular-shaped abandoned lot off Avenida Constitucion—one of the busier streets in the small town of Villa Unión. The lot rested between a bright pink taqueria and a dusty green stucco apartment building. Ever since the boys could remember, it had been home to their daily game. Every day after school they would don their gloves and play ball until dusk.

Danny threw his arm towards the plate, flicking his wrist on the release to make the ball arc, then drop.

The pitch started high and in. Diego Andujar, a stocky

fire hydrant of a boy, saw where the pitch was headed and ducked out of the way, careening out of the batter's box.

Mid-flight however, the pitch plunged low and moved in, whistling dead center over the plate and sending a plume of dust from the catcher's mitt.

"Strike three!" Danny said through a smile. "Quédate en la caja niña!" ("*Stay in the box little girl!*")

Diego wasn't amused, and scowled back as the players rotated positions, a new batter entering the box.

Danny was a big kid. At just fourteen years old, he stood a full six foot tall and weighed one hundred and eighty-five pounds. His jet-black hair poked out from beneath a tattered Dodgers cap, framing a boyish face with the hint of a mustache over his broad smile. He wore a black and gray striped shirt that hung over worn, blue jeans handed down from a cousin or neighbor. His family was poor, so clothing came from many places and the store was rarely one of them.

Danny frowned as he watched the sun drop lower and lower in the western sky. He called out to the group, "Guys, I gotta go."

Various grumbles came from the other boys—Danny was their best pitcher, after all—but each waved goodbye, then continued the game.

As he walked home, Danny dreamed of leaving the small town and going to the United States to play in the Majors. *One day,* he thought, *I'll pitch for the Dodgers or maybe even the Yankees.* But somewhere in the back of his mind he knew the reality of being a poor Mexican kid from a poor Mexican town. There just weren't many opportunities to be had. And odds were, he would end up working at one of the resorts in Mazatlán, or on a fishing boat that pulled tuna or shrimp from the Pacific Ocean.

For now, though, home was Villa Unión, a small city

thirty minutes east of Mazatlán. Perched on the banks of the Presidio River, it was poor by American standards. The streets, mostly dirt with patchy sections of cobblestone, were bracketed by all manner of homes and businesses, each painted in faded shades of green, blue, white, and pink.

Danny approached the entrance to the four-unit apartment building that had been his home for as long as he could remember. The building was two stories, white stucco with a faded blue trim, the entrance guarded by a white metal fence with a narrow gate in the center. A large brick-lined arch faced the street and illuminated a small landing on the second floor, where the Rincons lived.

The unit couldn't have been more than six hundred square feet. The front door opened into a rectangular living room crammed with a torn leather sofa facing an old set of kitchen cabinets repurposed to hold a twenty-seven-inch JVC television—not the flat screen variety. Right behind the sofa was a round wooden table with four mismatched chairs and a set of salt and pepper shakers, each shaped like a cat, one black one white.

The kitchen was cramped but functional. It had all the major amenities—refrigerator, stove and a sink that produced running water. Most of the time, anyway.

Next to the kitchen was a bathroom flanked by two bedrooms.

"Hola, Mom!" Danny shouted as he entered the apartment and headed for the bathroom to wash up.

The warm smell of fresh tortillas wafted through the air. Danny could see his mother fussing over a steaming pot of her famous Charro beans—a recipe handed down from her grandmother.

Anna Rincon carefully set the pot of beans onto the dining table. Still just thirty years old, she was an attractive woman with high cheekbones and deep brown eyes. Her hair was the color of dark Columbian coffee, and was pulled back in a tidy ponytail.

A single mother since she'd escaped her abusive ex-husband when Danny was a toddler, Anna often worked sixty hours a week in the laundry at the Casa Royale, a large tourist resort in Mazatlán. Her schedule, coupled with mothering a teenager, didn't allow much of a social life.

"Dinner's ready!" she called.

When Danny was seated, Anna returned to the table with a plate of fresh tortillas covered by a white linen towel and settled into her chair.

"How was school today?" she asked.

"It was fine."

"Well, did you learn anything?"

"I guess so," Danny replied.

"Tell me one thing you learned," Anna said, using her sternest motherly voice.

"Um ..." Danny fumbled, trying to remember the lessons from school that day. "Oh yeah, we learned about the Mexican Revolution in history class."

"And?"

"And how the people wanted to overthrow General Porfirio Diaz."

Anna smiled. "So, you *were* listening to your teacher."

Danny shrugged. "Yeah, most of the time."

Shifting the conversation to Danny's favorite topic, she asked, "And how was the game today?"

"Pretty good. I think I scared the beans out of Diego though," Danny said, grinning from ear to ear.

"That's not nice, Mijo." Anna scolded him. "I have to work with Diego's mother next week, and she's always complaining that the other boys pick on him."

"I know. I'll be nice to him tomorrow. It's just the way my

curveball works though." Danny grinned from ear to ear, this time with a hint of mischief in his smile.

Anna had no idea what a curveball was or how it worked, but seeing Danny's expression made her crack a guilty smile of her own. *Let Diego's mother complain,* she thought, beaming at the boy seated across the table.

---

Six miles away, a different kind of sit down was taking place inside the Villa Unión Produce Company, a regional distributor for tomatoes, green onions, and avocados.

A squatty white warehouse occupied most of the property, low and wide with streams of dirty rain staining the roofline. The building was surrounded by a ten-foot-tall fence, red metal bars spaced six inches apart and supported by rectangular concrete columns with rebar protruding from the top. Large tractor trailers lined the inside of the fence, waiting to be loaded with produce and taken to various destinations in Sinaloa.

It was the perfect place to transfer shipments of cocaine, marijuana, fentanyl—whatever the Cartel was moving at the time. The shipments would come up through Central America and be unloaded at cross docks like this one all over Mexico. At the cross dock the shipment would be broken down and hidden inside car parts, machinery, fertilizer or produce, then trucked over the border into the U.S.

The men sat in a small, dimly-lit office toward the back of the warehouse. Cheap wood paneling lined the walls, which were dotted by various awards for excellence in produce distribution. Miguel Alvarez sat on one side of a worn wooden desk while four cartel foot soldiers sat on the other.

Alvarez, a Lieutenant in the Sinaloa Cartel, had a notoriously short fuse and a violent temper. At just five foot six inches, he was small in stature, but cast an enormous shadow.

He wore a brown and white striped western shirt over black jeans. The custom-made alligator skin cowboy boots made him an inch or two taller and, although he'd never admit it, he liked that. His hair was slicked back, neatly making way for a pinched face with narrow eyes: an appearance that always made people feel like he was questioning their intent. Which, for the most part, he was.

"I want Felix Martin and the lab guarded at all times," he told the foot soldiers. "Two of you take the day shift, two of you the night shift."

The soldiers nodded. They were typical Cartel thugs. Young Mexican men sucked into a life of crime and violence by the promise of easy money and excitement. Alvarez knew the odds of these four making it to the age of thirty were slim. Foot soldiers seldom had the cunning to navigate the cutthroat world of the Sinaloa Cartel.

Yet Alvarez had to remind himself—he had come from similar beginnings. A boy of just twelve, he was plucked off the streets by one of the older kids and tasked with being a lookout. The older boys would sell drugs on the corner and the younger boys would patrol the area on bicycles, looking for policía.

As he grew older, he developed the street skills necessary to survive, and later thrive, within the organization.

His reputation was cemented at the ripe age of twenty-one when two other foot soldiers—brothers from Chihuahua—had snatched a large cash drop and fled in a stolen pickup truck. Tasked by his Lieutenant with finding the men, Alvarez knew this could be an opportunity to turn heads within leadership.

Forty-eight hours later, Alvarez had returned to the Lieutenant's office holding two duffel bags. The first contained the stolen cash—every cent of it. The second contained the heads of the two traitors. Both sets of eyes had been removed, blood dripping from the empty sockets.

As he had hoped, the endeavor *did* turn heads among leadership. Soon, Alvarez became the second in command for a Lieutenant that controlled Durango, a large state East of Sinaloa. Eventually, he became a Lieutenant himself—an honor given to him personally by the big boss, Arturo Aguado, whom everyone simply called "Jefe."

"This is a very important project," Alvarez finished instructing the soldiers. "Jefe will be watching closely, so don't screw this up. Any questions?"

"No, boss." Each man answered, then stood and headed out of the office.

# CHAPTER 2

After his demotion from the majors, the next five years proved to be a slow spiral into anonymity and depression for Dillon Reynolds. He bounced from one team to the next. One small town to the next. One uncomfortable bus ride to the next.

His current team, an Independent League club called the Bridge City Drillers, were on a seven-game losing streak. Two weeks ago, a more attractive league had poached four of their best players and the remaining talent, if you could call it that, was marginal at best.

Tonight marked the third game of a four-game home stand, the ninth inning coming and going shortly after Reynolds' final strikeout. The result was loss number eight in a row.

A 10-7 defeat to the Beaumont Oil Kings.

Players began filing through the dugout, down a narrow concrete tunnel to the locker room where there were four rows of shabby green metal lockers. On the opposite side of the lockers sat a large communal shower that spouted luke-warm water from calcified shower heads. A short hall behind the shower led to two additional rooms.

The first was a gray-tiled bathroom with a cluster of urinals and stalls, opposite a bank of white porcelain sinks mounted beneath a large mirror. Across from the bathroom was a small, dingy manager's office cluttered with books, papers, and tidbits of baseball memorabilia—typical décor for a minor league manager's office.

Reynolds slumped down in front of the locker where his street clothes hung, replaying another lackluster performance. Before he could manage the top button on his jersey, a voice barked out "Reynolds!"

The call came from the dingy Manager's office.

"Come see me."

Reynolds got up slowly knowing this couldn't be good news. He shuffled down the hall, cleats clacking across the concrete floor.

As he entered the room Reynolds saw the team's manager, Jack McKinnon, hunched behind a small wooden desk looking over a spiral-bound book of score sheets. Jack insisted on personally keeping a log of each game, said it helped him stay in tune with the players. Whatever that meant.

"Have a seat," McKinnon said, not bothering to look up from the book.

Reynolds eased his large frame into a metal folding chair. "How's it going Jack?"

McKinnon, it seemed, was in no mood for conversation. He simply said, "You've been cut."

"What?" Reynolds asked, feigning surprise—knowing he should have been cut weeks ago.

McKinnon looked up wearily from the score sheet and his voice softened. "Dillon, you're a good kid, but you're just not progressing in your career."

Reynolds had seen this movie before.

"Look at it this way," he continued. "Everything happens

for a reason. You could try to catch on with another club next year. This doesn't have to be the end of the road."

But in his heart of hearts, Reynolds knew this *was* the end of the road. His love and passion for the game had been slowly dying over the last five years, and this moment was the culminating death knell.

"Jack?" Reynolds asked hesitantly. "What did you do when after the game passed you by?"

McKinnon leaned back in his chair and removed his black framed reading glasses. "I got angry," he said. "I was pissed that I hadn't accomplished everything I wanted to do in the game. I felt cheated, and it ate me up for a couple years."

"How'd you right the ship?" Reynolds asked, hoping for some meaningful piece of advice to cling to.

"I decided to give back." McKinnon answered. "I started volunteered at coaching clinics for kids. After a while, I realized I loved what I was doing. It eventually rebuilt my love for the game. Now helping develop young players is more rewarding to me than my playing career ever was." He must have seen the look of skepticism on Reynolds' face, because he added, "I know, from where you're sitting, it doesn't sound like a solution. But it worked for me. Don't see why it couldn't work for you."

The words rang hollow for Reynolds. Being around kids was the last thing he wanted to do right now. Nonetheless, he nodded and smiled anyway. "Thanks Jack, maybe I'll give that a shot."

―――――

That evening, Reynolds stretched out across a grungy plaid couch in the apartment he shared with Jimmy Hernandez, a fresh faced second baseman from the University of Texas.

The second-floor apartment was a two-bedroom, one bath unit with a galley kitchen, a small living room and a narrow deck perched outside a sliding glass door.

Reynolds stared out through the glass to the parking lot below, thinking, *What now?* He was 26 years old. No college education. No actual skills of any kind other than baseball. And it appeared even that had failed him now.

His finances weren't in great shape. He'd spent most of the signing bonus Arizona had given him. And while he could make it last for a while, coasting along and living off the last of his savings didn't chalk up to a plan in his mind.

At the very least, he had to find a new place to live. The apartment was leased by the team, and they'd given him twenty-four hours to pack up his stuff and move out.

The sound of keys jiggling in the lock roused him from his thoughts.

Jimmy Hernandez strode in, a backpack over his right shoulder. "Hey Dillon," he said, a somber look on his face. "I heard about you getting cut. I'm sorry, man."

"Ah, don't worry about it. I'll catch on somewhere else next year." Reynolds lied.

"Anything I can do?" Jimmy asked.

"Not unless you've got a spare apartment. I have to be out of here tomorrow."

"I actually might," Jimmy replied. "My uncle runs a baseball academy. I used to help him out sometimes. Pay isn't great, but you get room and board. You want his number?"

"Sure, why not?"

Jimmy pulled a phone from his pocket and shared his uncle's contact info.

Reynolds' phone buzzed, and the contact lit up his screen. It read, *Eduardo 'Ed' Hernandez, Sinaloa Baseball Academy.*

"Sinaloa?" Reynolds asked. "Where's that?"

"Mexico." Jimmy replied. "The Academy is near Mazatlán. A lot of the top Latin American prospects go there for training during the fall and winter."

"Thanks Jimmy, maybe I'll give him a call," Reynolds said, thinking back to his conversation with Jack McKinnon, earlier in the day.

Jimmy nodded. "No problem. I'm going to call it a night. McKinnon's in a bad mood so we're having early workouts tomorrow."

"Good luck," Reynolds replied, as Jimmy disappeared into his bedroom.

Reynolds didn't believe in coincidences. He thought back to what McKinnon had said about giving back. He hadn't ever done that, really. He'd always been so focused on his own career he'd never even thought of helping someone else.

Maybe this thing in Mexico could work—help him figure out what to do next. Of course, it could also be a huge mistake. What did he know about working with kids? Either way, he didn't have a lot of other options.

"Here goes nothing," he said, sighing as he dialed the number for Ed Hernandez.

A voice on the other end answered: "Baseball Academy."

"I'm looking for Ed Hernandez," Reynolds said.

"Speaking."

"Hi Ed, my name is Dillon. I'm a friend of your nephew Jimmy. He said you might need some help at the Academy this fall."

"You have any coaching experience?" Hernandez asked.

"No." Reynolds replied. "But I spent some time in the Majors, and I've been around the game for years."

"What'd you say your name was?" Hernandez asked.

"Dillon. Dillon Reynolds."

Hernandez's voice went an octave higher. "Dillon Reynolds from the Diamondbacks?"

"More recently of the Bridge City Drillers," Reynolds quipped. "But yeah, I spent some time with the Diamondbacks."

"Amigo, I remember that September you had a few years back." He let out a long, slow whistle. "You lit it up like the fourth of July."

"Yeah, it was a fun time," Reynolds replied sheepishly.

"How's the eye?"

"It's fine. About the position though…"

"Yeah, I've got a spot for you. I could definitely use another hitting coach."

"Great," Reynolds said. "When would you like me to start?"

"Honestly, I could use you yesterday. We've got kids coming in from all over and I need help getting them settled. There are scouts from a half dozen clubs coming in towards the beginning of December and I want the boys to be ready."

Reynolds paused. He didn't think he'd be needed so soon. "I need a day or two to tie up some loose ends here, but I could be there by the end of the week."

"Alright then," Hernandez said, shuffling papers in the background. "I'll have my office manager give you a call to set up travel arrangements. We'll cover your airfare and set you up with a place to stay while you're here."

"Sounds good," Reynolds replied. "I'll see you in a few days—and thank you for the opportunity, Ed."

As he set down the phone, a small surge of optimism swept through Reynolds' mind.

"Hmm," he muttered to himself. "Maybe everything does happen for a reason."

# CHAPTER 3

Reynolds arrived at the Academy just after two in the afternoon.

The facility was more impressive than he had imagined. It was a modern, L-shaped building with floor to ceiling glass windows lining the ground level. Cube-shaped architectural panels lined the top of the building, forming a tall white cap over the structure.

Reynolds exited the taxi, sunlight flooding his vision. He winced slightly and blinked his injured eye. Sensitivity to sudden, bright light was a side effect that would probably be with him for the rest of his life.

As he approached a small, cylindrical guard shack, a man in dark slacks and a white security uniform emerged. "Hola."

"My name is Dillon Reynolds," he said, hoping the man understood English. "I'm here to see Ed Hernandez."

"Sí." The man returned to the guard shack.

A moment later, the green metal gate behind the guard shack slid open and the guard once again emerged from the shack. "Señor Hernandez will meet you at the reception desk."

The lobby mirrored the clean, modern look of the building's exterior. Decorated like an interactive museum, the walls were lined with three-dimensional artwork shaped like baseball bats and catcher's masks. Other walls featured colorful murals of Latin American greats like Clemente, Marichal and Pujols. A series of screens formed a floating cube over the center of the room, playing highlights of classic World Series games. It was all very impressive.

"Dillon?" a voice called out behind him.

Reynolds turned to see a man approaching. He was about Reynolds' height but thirty pounds heavier and twenty-five years older. His face was weathered, eyes squinted from years in the sun. A large handlebar mustache gave him the look of a character from an old Western. He wore gray cotton shorts, a black t-shirt and a black baseball cap, all featuring the stylized A.B.S. that formed the logo for the "Academia de Béisbol de Sinaloa."

"Eduardo Hernandez," the man said, sticking out his hand. "But call me Ed."

"Nice to meet you, Ed," Dillon replied, shaking the man's hand.

"Flight in was good?" Hernandez asked.

"Yeah, it's a short hop from Houston."

"I'd like to get you settled in today so you can hit the ground running tomorrow. I've got six players coming in from the Dominican in the morning, and I'll need your help to get them registered."

"Sounds like a plan." Reynolds replied, following Hernandez to a set of stainless-steel elevator doors at the back of the room.

As they approached the elevators, Hernandez pointed to his left. "This wing of the building houses the dorms for the players, classrooms, a lounge area, and a cafeteria. The other side of the building is where you'll be staying. Along with living quarters for the staff, there's a section of offices for coaches and administrative staff. The rest of the space is used for training—batting cages, weight room, an indoor practice field and a locker room. Behind the building are two full-sized fields."

Both men stepped into the elevator and headed to the second floor. As the doors parted, they began down a long hallway. The corridor led to a sky bridge between the two wings of the building and gave an impressive view of the city below.

"Your room is right over here, Amigo." Hernandez gestured down another hallway to his left. "Room number twenty. I left a training manual with instructions on what to do tomorrow, as well as some general info on the Academy. Breakfast starts at six and I recommend you get there early. The players will pick the cafeteria clean if you're late. After breakfast we'll have a quick staff meeting, then get to work."

Hernandez turned back toward the elevator. "I'm teaching a bunting clinic at three, so this is where I'll leave you for today. Glad to have you aboard, Amigo."

"Glad to be here," Reynolds replied.

Room number twenty was small and stark. There was no colorful artwork like he'd seen in the lobby. A twin bed rested against one wall, fitted with a green blanket stretched tight around the corners. A narrow wooden desk sat against the opposite wall, with a matching chair tucked neatly beneath. Sitting atop the desk was a thick three-ring binder full of training notes and other information.

Reynolds plopped his bag on the floor and reached for the binder. It was heavy and contained hundreds of pages.

The first sheet was a welcome letter to new employees. Quickly scanning the letter, Reynolds turned to the next page. EMPLOYEE TRAINING MANUAL was printed in all caps across the top of the page, along with the A.B.S. logo stamped proudly beneath it.

Flipping through the pages in the binder, Reynolds could tell he had a lot to absorb. He grabbed the only pillow on the bed and propped it up against the headboard. *Going to be a long night,* he thought, and began flipping through the pages.

---

"Give me an update on the project," Arturo Aguado barked, forgoing any pleasantries.

Aguado's study was lavish—even as drug lords went. A gilt wood desk sat in front of a massive marble fireplace while two glowing Baccarat Crystal chandeliers hung from the ceiling and bathed the room in a warm glow. A large Savonnerie carpet lined the floor, boasting fanciful clusters of gold and red flowers that danced against its black woolen background.

Miguel Alvarez and Felix Martin sat on opposite ends of a grand Rococo-style sofa, facing Aguado as he continued: "You told me twelve months, and it's been almost eighteen." He pointed at Martin.

Aguado was almost sixty-five years old—ancient for a drug lord, and each year he seemed to become a little less patient than the last. He wore a heavily starched white button-up shirt and dark slacks pressed to perfection. His salt and pepper hair was combed back, exposing a pronounced forehead, seemingly supported by a pair of large bushy eyebrows.

"The formula has proven to be a bit trickier than we thought Jefe," But my theory is solid. I just need a little more time." Felix Martin replied, his ruddy cheeks giving his face a boyish quality to which a badly receding hairline immediately contradicted.

"You've been saying that for weeks, Felix."

"But Jefe, you couldn't begin to understand how difficult this is," Martin said, immediately regretting his arrogant tone.

Aguado stopped pacing and narrowed his eyes at Martin, gently swirling a crystal tumbler of tequila in his right hand. "Is that a fact, Mr. Martin? You think I'm too stupid to understand, do you?"

Martin began stumbling and stuttering. "N ... no Jefe. I just, well, I mean, it's really complica ..."

Without warning, Aguado threw the contents of the glass into Martin's face and watched as the tequila dripped from his eyes and nose, down his chin and onto the lavish rug.

"I want progress and I want it now." Aguado's voice lowered to a hiss. "Because if you can't produce, I have no use for you. Do you know what that means, Mr. Martin?"

The chemist nodded slowly as a wave of anxiety swept through his body.

"You've got two weeks." Aguado spat the words at Martin. He was losing faith in both the chemist and the project.

Martin's heart dropped. "Jefe, that's just not enough time." He pled.

Aguado shot Martin another steely glare. "Two. Weeks," he said, annunciating slowly. "I would get to work if I were you."

Martin could feel his stomach tighten and begin to spasm as he rose from the sofa, his shirt now drenched with tequila. "I'll do my best, Jefe."

A long second passed as Martin awkwardly left the study, head lowered like a beaten dog.

"Think he'll get it done?" Alvarez asked Aguado.

"I don't know Miguel. But it's time for this tree to produce fruit or be cut down to make way for another. Either way, I'm done waiting."

―――

The baseball pinged off the aluminum bat and whizzed sharply over Reynolds' head. The kid could hit. At just five foot eight inches tall and one hundred fifty pounds, Alejandro Avila wasn't a power hitter, but he made contact with virtually every pitch that was remotely around the strike zone. That, coupled with his silky-smooth fielding skills, made him a hot commodity in baseball circles.

But that was true of many boys here. They were all excellent ball players. Reynolds had been thoroughly impressed with the level of talent he'd seen over his first week at the Academy.

He thought about the dreams and hopes these kids must have. Dreams of making it to the Majors one day. Signing big contracts and providing for their families back home. It brought him back to his own early days, the promise *his* career had once held.

A loud buzzer roused him from thought, signaling the end of batting practice. The boys gathered up their gear and began talking and laughing as they headed toward the cafeteria for dinner.

Reynolds was hungry as well, and it was Taco Tuesday at the cafeteria, if he remembered right. His mouth watered—tacos would hit the spot.

Ed Hernandez had just finished throwing batting practice in a nearby cage and called out when he saw Reynolds gathering his things:

"Dillon, where you headed?"

"Cafeteria." Reynolds replied. "I'm a sucker for tacos."

"Me too, but I'm a sucker for everything." Hernandez said, patting his round belly with a grin. "You want to get some real street tacos? There's a place thirty minutes from here that makes the world's best Al Pastor."

"I'm game," said Reynolds. "I don't have any other batting practice sessions scheduled for today."

Hernandez slung an equipment bag over his shoulder. "Great, meet me out front in ten."

Hernandez drove a white Range Rover with large black wheels and a red leather interior. *The Academy must do pretty well,* Reynolds thought as they sped down the highway.

"What do you think of the program so far?" Hernandez asked.

"Impressive," Reynolds said. "The facilities, the staff, the players—all top-notch."

"Good, I'm glad you like it. I started the Academy twenty years ago after my playing career fizzled out and it's been my life's work ever since. It was tough going at first, trying to make a name for myself and the Academy, but I made some sacrifices and got the place to where it is today. Did you know we've produced twenty-seven major league ball players over the last ten years?"

"I had no idea," Dillon replied. "But I'm not surprised. The level of talent in that building is off the charts."

"Yes, it is." Hernandez beamed like a proud papa. "Here's the place up ahead."

Dillon spotted the building right away. It stood out like a sore thumb. The bright pink walls were trimmed in an even brighter shade of yellow. A large mural covered the balcony wall on the second floor, featuring a colorful Mexican countryside with the words *La Taqueria* hand-painted across the center.

Hernandez pulled to the side of the narrow street and

parked in front of the building. As they exited the vehicle, Reynolds noticed a group of boys playing baseball in the vacant lot next door. "Is this lunch or a scouting trip?" he asked jokingly.

"Just lunch," Hernandez replied. "But it never hurts to keep your eyes open."

As advertised, the tacos were the best Reynolds had ever tasted. Expertly cut from a rotating spit, the tangy pork resonated with flavors of cumin, guajillo chilis, fresh pineapple and cilantro.

After four tacos, Reynolds put his hands up in mock surrender. "I need to tap out. I can't eat another thing."

"And?" Hernandez asked.

"Best I've ever had—and I'm a bit of a connoisseur," Reynolds replied with a satisfied smile.

Hernandez smiled back. "Glad you like them." He rose and put his napkin on the table. "I'm going to use the restroom, then we'll head back."

As Hernandez started for the restrooms, Reynolds strolled out of the Taqueria onto the street. He heard laughing nearby and remembered the boys playing baseball. Never one to miss a game, he turned the corner and leaned against the wall of the restaurant, giving him a view of the vacant lot.

The pitcher was a big kid, maybe sixteen years old by the look of him. He wore an old Dodgers cap and a well-used Wilson glove on his right hand—a southpaw.

He watched the boy wind up and fire a fastball straight down the middle. The batter missed badly, and the ball thundered into the catcher's glove.

*Damn!* Reynolds thought, taken aback by the pitch.

Another wind up, another fastball. Again, the batter missed badly. *That had to be eighty-five, ninety miles an hour!* Reynolds thought. *What else you got, kid?*

Reynolds now watched intently. The catcher had flashed a single finger on the first two pitches but now held down three fingers. Dodger's cap wound up and flicked his wrist towards the plate. The batter, expecting another fastball, swung wildly in front of the pitch, missing by a mile as the ball rose in the air then plummeted into the catcher's glove.

Without thinking, Reynolds said, "No way!" Apparently louder than he'd intended, too, as the boys all turned to look in his direction.

A hand clamped his shoulder from behind. "Ready?" Hernandez asked.

"Hold on. You should see this kid throw."

"We've got to get back. I've got a meeting I can't miss." Hernandez circled to the driver's side of the Range Rover. "We'll come back another time."

Back in his room that evening, Reynolds thumbed through the schedule for the following day. His thoughts wandered, though, and he couldn't seem to get the kid in the Dodgers hat out of his head.

*Was the kid really that good, or is my vision getting even worse?* Reynolds asked himself.

It was true that, after the accident, his vision had never returned to normal, but still. Reynolds quickly put the thought out of his head. No, he knew a good thing when he saw it—this kid threw heat. And that curveball? Nasty. If he was half as good as he seemed, the boy might be a good prospect for the Academy.

Reynolds mulled over the notion for a moment. *I'll just have to go back,* he thought. *I'll grab Ed later in the week and we'll go scout him out.*

# CHAPTER 4

He never got tired of this view. The emerald-green grass, the rust-colored infield dirt—even the powdery white chalk outlining the batter's boxes. Reynolds had spent thousands of hours on fields like this one, and it felt like home.

"Turn two, turn two!" he called out, leaning over the padded green railing of the dugout.

Reynolds watched as the shortstop deftly fielded the ground ball and flipped it to the second baseman. The second baseman jumped out of the way of a sliding base runner and threw the ball across his body to the outstretched glove of the first baseman.

It was a perfectly executed double play and, once again, Reynolds marveled at the talent in front of him.

The Friday afternoon scrimmage was a ritual at the Academy—a fun way for the boys to cap off the week.

The two players that had the best week of practice, as judged by the coaches, got to be captains. They would each take turns picking players until the teams were full. Red team vs. green team.

Today, Reynolds was coaching the green team while Ed

Hernandez coached the red team. The double play had punctuated, a 10-run drubbing by Reynolds' green team, and the players joked and laughed as they retrieved their bats and gloves from the dugout.

Reynolds approached Hernandez, who stood in the batter's box, bat in hand. He was giving a final bit of advice to the boy that had grounded into the double play. "You can't pull an outside pitch," he said. "You have to go with the pitch. Push it to right field."

The boy nodded and Hernandez patted him on the back. "You'll get it, Juan. Just keep working," he said, as Reynolds watched.

"The boys are looking pretty good out there," Reynolds said.

Never satisfied, Hernandez replied, "Yeah, there's still a lot of work to do before the scouts get here in December. We really don't have much time."

It was mid-October, a full six weeks before the scouts would arrive, yet Hernandez still acted as though they were two runs down in the bottom of the ninth inning. Reynolds admired his dedication to perfection.

"You want to grab some of those famous tacos for dinner tonight?" Reynolds asked, secretly hoping they would get to see the kid in the Dodgers hat again.

"Can't today. I've got a meeting in the city, and it might take a while."

"No problem. Maybe next time."

As Reynolds turned to leave, Hernandez called after him, "If you want to go solo, you can borrow one of the utility trucks. I can drop a set of keys for you at the front desk."

"That'd be great Ed," Dillon said, looking back. "Those tacos are calling my name!"

Twenty minutes later, Reynolds sped down the highway

toward *La Taqueria*. The rundown utility truck didn't ride nearly as nice as Ed's Range Rover, and each bump in the road caused him to bounce off the worn bench seat a fraction of an inch.

As he approached the restaurant, Reynolds saw just what he was hoping to see—the boy in the Dodgers hat. This time, instead of standing on the mound, the boy was in the batter's box. Or, more aptly, the patch of dirt with the fewest weeds.

Reynolds let the truck idle a moment in the street, watching as the pitcher wound up and let the ball fly. The pitch was inside, and the boy turned on it sharply, ripping the ball into a chain-link fence on the side of the restaurant. On a regulation field, it would've easily been a stand-up double.

*He can hit too,* Reynolds thought, remembering himself at that age. *A real five tool player.*

Reynolds switched off the ignition and stepped out of the truck. Inside the restaurant, he ordered four of the Al Pastor tacos, this time bringing them to the small patio in front of the taqueria. There were two weather-worn, high top tables in front of the building, and he dragged one to where he had a good vantage point to watch the game.

Dodgers Hat was back on the mound, and Reynolds watched intently as the boy hurled four heavy fastballs in a row. Not only did the pitches look good, they sounded the part—popping into the catcher's glove. He'd heard that sound hundreds of times in the pros, but never in high school, which was probably the right age range for this kid.

Finishing the last of his four tacos, Reynolds crumpled up the wax paper wrapper and piled it on the plate with the others. As he looked up from the plate, he heard a loud *ting* and saw a foul ball from the corner of his good eye. It was on a crash course with Reynolds' face, and he instinctively stuck out his hand, catching the ball before it could make impact.

It had been a while since he'd caught a hot shot like that bare-handed. In high school, he'd been on the mound when a batter hit a line drive up the middle. Knowing he couldn't get his glove across his body in time to catch the ball, Reynolds had stuck out his right hand. Much like then, his palm now stung and pulsed red.

"You okay man?" called a voice. Dodgers Hat was walking toward him.

"No big deal," Reynolds assured him, almost glad the ball had come his way, so he had an excuse to talk to the kid. "What's your name?"

"Danny."

"Danny, you're a heck of a ballplayer. Who do you play for?"

The boy looked confused for a moment, then said, "No one. We just play here after school."

Reynolds shook his head. Now he was the one looking confused. "You've never played organized baseball?"

"My school doesn't have a team," the boy explained. "They only have one for soccer."

"Then where'd you learn to pitch?"

A smile overtook the kid's face. "YouTube."

Reynolds couldn't help but laugh out loud. "You're one of a kind, Danny. How old are you?"

"Fourteen," the boy replied.

From his stature, Reynolds thought the boy had to have been at least sixteen. He'd never even heard of a fourteen-year-old that could throw as hard as this kid.

He handed the ball back to the boy. "My name is Dillon Reynolds. I work at the Academia de Béisbol de Sinaloa. We train ..."

Danny quickly cut over him. "I know all about the Academy. It's where the best prospects go to train." He proceeded to list a half dozen big leaguers that had been through the program.

"You know the Academy, huh?"

Danny nodded. "Everyone around here does."

"How would you like to come and try out?"

Danny's eyes widened to the size of dinner plates. "You serious? You want me to come to the Academy for a tryout?"

Reynolds was having fun now. "Yeah, unless you're busy."

"No ... I mean, how ... when is the tryout?" Danny stammered.

"How about tomorrow?" Reynolds replied. "Ten o'clock?"

Danny's face turned serious. "I'll have to ask my mom."

"Of course." Reynolds assured him. "If she's okay with it, we'll see you both tomorrow morning. If not ..." His voice trailed off.

"I'll be there!" Danny replied and pounded the ball in his glove. "Thank you, Mr. Reynolds!"

Reynolds smiled as the boy returned to the game. He couldn't wait to see what the kid was capable of.

―――

It had been ten long days since the meeting with Aguado and Felix Martin had worked nonstop ever since. He'd barely slept, and his eyes carried drooping bags that made him look wraithlike in the bright lights of the laboratory. Food was an afterthought over the past week, with Martin only wolfing down the odd frozen burrito or bag of chips.

Against Aguado's wishes, he'd sent the other two chemists away at the beginning of the week. They were more of a nuisance now anyway, and Martin figured that, if it was his life that was on the line, he would run the show his way.

Now, surrounded by the persistent hum of the lab equipment, he marveled at the computer screen before him. He'd done it. As General George Patton had said, "Pressure makes diamonds." And the pharmaceutical formulation in front of him was the Hope Diamond of opiates.

Martin exhaled slowly, flooded with relief as he stared at the computer screen. How had he gotten this far off the beaten path? Sitting alone in an illicit drug lab in the middle of Mexico. A far cry from where he started.

Once, Martin had been a rising star in the chemistry world. He'd taken a job as a pharmaceutical chemist with Johnson Pharmaceuticals in Houston, Texas, straight out of MIT. There, he'd risen quickly up the ladder thanks to his groundbreaking work developing a series of revolutionary new therapeutic agents that made the company millions.

But as his reputation grew, so did his taste for gambling away his paycheck at the track. First, it was just a weekend trip here or there—a good time with friends throwing a couple of bucks on the ponies. Over time, however, Martin became convinced his brilliance went beyond chemistry into the realm of horse racing.

He began to study every facet of the sport, researching horses, jockeys, owners, and trainers. He would read and reread every piece of information he could get his hands on, more and more convinced he could develop a formula that would consistently predict winners. Every loss was simply another tweak to the formula. Eventually, he would get it right. He knew he could crack the code. He just needed more time.

But time was money, and the setbacks had begun to stack up. His salary no longer covered the extensive losses.

Martin began taking loans from one of the hustlers at the track—small at first, larger over time.

Within six months he'd racked up a balance of fifteen thousand dollars, making minimum payments and watching the vig compound over and over.

Work suffered from his maniacal addiction. His co-workers complained about his poor attitude and erratic behavior. The sick days were piling up as well—a dozen in three months. There were warnings from his superiors, constant reprimands, even offers to assist with treatment, but Martin had ignored the warnings and shunned the help.

Eventually, on a sweltering Friday in July, Martin was unceremoniously fired and escorted out of the building.

He tried over and over to get a position with another lab, but word of his gambling addiction had spread quickly through the pharmaceutical community, and everyone shut their doors.

Now, with his comfortable salary gone, it was becoming more and more difficult to feed his addiction. With his gambling debt comfortably in the five-figure range, the loan shark was getting antsy and wanted his money now—all of it. Martin tried to dodge the man when he could, but eventually there was nowhere to run.

It was then that the two men from the cartel showed up at his door, claiming they had purchased his debt.

After the second visit, the two men had taken him to the back room of a small check cashing store in southwest Houston. There, the men explained they were members of the Sinaloa Cartel, and told him about a product called Azúcar *Sugar*.

The product was nicknamed Azúcar because it looked and tasted just like ordinary table sugar. If a shipment from Mexico got searched at the U.S. border, it would pass any inspection with flying colors. But when diluted in a small amount of ethyl alcohol and ingested, the substance produced heroin-like effects—and at a fraction of the cost.

Azúcar would completely turn the world of drug trafficking on its head, leaving rival cartels and DEA operatives helpless in its wake.

It was a brilliant idea in theory. Except the formula wasn't working as intended. The cartel's chemists were educated men, but they didn't have Felix Martin's MIT pedigree, or his knack for creating ground-breaking formulations.

When news of Felix Martin and his gambling troubles had reached Aguado, the drug lord didn't hesitate to sink his claws into the brilliant chemist so the man could *repay his debt*. The cartel had flown him to Mazatlán and built a lab to Martin's exacting specifications, sparing neither money nor manpower.

Now, here he was—alone in the lab. The formula was complete. Jefe would be pleased.

Martin slipped a small thumb drive into the USB port on his computer and downloaded the file. He would take this to Aguado personally, along with a sample of the product. And this time, he wouldn't be leaving the meeting like a reprimanded dog.

———

On his walk home, Danny didn't know if his feet ever touched the ground. He was sure he'd simply floated back to the apartment, his big-league dreams suddenly a thousand miles closer than they had been yesterday.

*No,* he told himself. *Don't get your hopes up.*

But he couldn't contain his excitement. The Academy had been the start for so many great players. He thought of donning the Dodger blue or Yankee pinstripes. Getting the final strikeout in the World Series. Even making it to Cooperstown.

Inside the apartment, Danny took his position on an imaginary mound. "Full count, two outs in the bottom of the ninth." His voice lowered, trying to mimic the play-by-play announcers from television.

"Here's the windup—and the pitch."

Danny wound up and threw an invisible fastball, envisioning the batter swinging and missing. He pumped his fist in the air. "Strike three! The Dodgers win the World Series!"

Danny gazed into the imaginary stands and saw his mother, clapping loudly with a proud smile across her face.

The thought of his mother tugged him back to the present. *First things first.* He thought. *I've got to talk mom into letting me try out.*

Anna Rincon was working later than usual this Friday, and wouldn't be home until eight o'clock in the evening. She'd be tired and possibly grumpy from the long day, so Danny knew he had to do something nice for her. A little brown nosing never hurt anyone.

With less than an hour before his mother's return, Danny reached into his pocket and pulled out twenty-five pesos. He hoped the small pile of coins would be enough, then headed out the front door toward the corner market.

He reached the small store with lightning speed, bursting through the door and startling the woman behind the counter.

"Do you sell flowers here?" he asked.

The woman pointed to a metal stand in the corner of the market, where brightly colored bundles of Dahlias exploded in hues of pink, red, yellow and purple.

"How much?" Danny asked.

"Two hundred pesos."

He didn't have anywhere near that and suddenly felt desperation welling up inside him.

Sensing his despair, the woman behind the counter called to him, "We have single flowers for twenty pesos."

"Perfect!" He slammed the small pile of coins on the counter, again making the woman jump a little.

The trip home was even faster than the trip to the market. Danny carefully placed the single Dahlia in a glass of water and set it on the table. *A nice centerpiece*, he thought.

Shifting gears, he entered the small kitchen and began phase two of the "butter up mom" mission.

One of his mother's favorite meals was traditional Mexican Chilaquiles, a wonderful combination of fried tortilla strips topped with scrambled eggs, tangy green sauce and Cotija cheese. Aside from being one of his mother's favorites, it was also very easy to make. A win-win.

Danny quickly set about frying the tortillas and cooking the scrambled eggs. His mother usually made the green sauce from scratch, but he didn't have time for that. The bottled kind from the refrigerator would have to do.

His timing proved to be perfect. Danny began plating the Chilaquiles as he heard the creak of the apartment's front door.

Stepping inside, Anna immediately recognized the familiar scent of fried tortillas. "Something smells good in here," she called to the kitchen.

She knew Danny rarely cooked for her. And when he did, it was because he wanted something.

Anna set her purse on the worn leather couch and approached the table. "And flowers?" she asked, seeing the crimson-colored Dahlia in the center of the table.

Finishing off the entrees, Danny spread a few crumbles of cheese over each plate and set them carefully on the table.

"Sit down mom. You must be tired."

Anna eyed him suspiciously as she plopped into a chair. "What's all this for?"

"No reason. Just thought you'd be hungry after work."

Now she was even more suspicious. "Daniel Antonio Rincon." Anna always used his full name when she meant business. "What are you up to?"

Danny could no longer contain his excitement, or his secret. "A coach from the Sinaloa Baseball Academy saw me playing ball today and wants me to come to the school for a tryout tomorrow!"

"Tomorrow?" Anna asked. "You know that's my only day off this week, and I have to run some errands around town."

Undeterred, Danny continued. "It won't take long—maybe a couple hours."

"Mijo," Anna replied, "You know how these things work. It costs a lot of money to go to those schools."

"He didn't say anything about money, mom. Besides, it's just a tryout. I probably won't make it, anyway."

Danny could see his mother's wheels turning as she crunched a bite of tortilla and egg.

After what seemed like an eternity, his mother replied, "Fine. We'll go to the tryout. You'll have to help me run errands after, though."

"No problem!" Danny replied enthusiastically.

His voice softened, and he said, "Thanks mom. I know how much you already do for me."

"You're welcome, Mijo," she replied, a smile beginning to bend across her lips. "The Chilaquiles are delicious."

## CHAPTER 5

It was Saturday at the Academy, which meant no organized baseball activities. The boys would get the weekend off to catch up on homework or visit with friends and family. The staff would use the time to take care of personal errands and start planning for the week ahead.

Inside the cafeteria, Dillon Reynolds and Ed Hernandez sat opposite each other on a long narrow lunch table, each sipping a steaming cup of coffee.

"I'm impressed with the work you're doing here, Dillon," Hernandez said. "The boys really respond to your coaching style."

"*Coaching style?*" Reynolds chuckled. "I didn't know I had one."

"Know it or not, you do. I've seen many coaches come and go over the years. And the good ones all have one thing in common—they connect with the kids. Anyone can teach the mechanics of a good swing or proper fielding techniques, but a good coach knows his players and teaches the information in a way each player will best understand."

Reynolds took a minute to process the advice. It was true he connected well with the kids—an unexpected development. He marveled at how they weren't yet tainted by the struggles of life. They were fresh canvases, and their youthful exuberance seemed to take his mind away from his own problems.

"I still feel like I'm winging it, Ed. But I honestly enjoy the work. It's ..."

Hernandez cut him off. "Rewarding?" He sipped his coffee, wearing a wry smile.

"Yeah, I guess it is." It was somewhat of a revelation. Reynolds hadn't done something rewarding in a long, long time. He took a sip of coffee. "Speaking of rewarding, do you remember the kid I mentioned? The one outside the Taqueria?"

"Vaguely," Hernandez admitted.

"Well, the other day when I went back to get tacos, he was playing ball again. The kid is lights out, Ed. He throws hard. And his curve is wicked."

"And you're telling me this because?"

"Because I invited him to come to the Academy so we could get a better look at him. Maybe have him throw to some of the boys."

"I don't mean to burst your bubble Dillon, but he's literally a kid off the street. These boys will eat him alive."

"I'm not sure about that, Ed. I think the kid's got something special. I'll bet you twenty bucks he can strikeout Avila."

"Alejandro?" Hernandez replied incredulously. "No way."

"Fifty bucks," Reynolds shot back.

Hernandez laughed and threw up his hands. "Okay, okay. If you feel that strongly, let's take a look at him."

"Great, he'll be here at ten."

The wry smile returned to Hernandez's face as he shook his head. "You don't waste any time, do you, amigo?"

"No sir," Reynolds replied, matching the older man's grin.

---

The rusty Toyota Corolla rolled to a stop in front of the small cylindrical guard shack, its brakes groaning out a tired squeal. Anna Rincon rolled down the window as a man in a security uniform approached the car.

"Can I help you?" the guard asked.

"Yes, we're here to see Dillon Reynolds," Anna replied.

The guard returned to the shack, and moments later emerged as the gate behind it slid open.

"Visitor parking is to your right. From there you'll see signs that point to the lobby."

"Thank you." Anna eased the car forward through the gate.

"Pretty fancy, huh, mom?" Danny said to his mother. He'd seen the Academy from the street but had never been inside the gates.

"Yes, but who do you think pays for all this, Mijo? If they ask us for money, you know we can't afford it."

"I know, mom. But I still want to try out. Like I said, I probably won't make it, anyway."

"And that's just fine," Anna said. "School is more important, anyway."

As they stepped through the entrance to the lobby, a voice called out, "Hey, Danny!"

It was Dillon Reynolds, the man he'd spoken to yesterday.

"Hey, Dillon," Danny replied.

"Is this your mom?" Reynolds asked.

Anna stuck out her hand. "Yes, I'm Anna Rincon."

"Nice to meet you, Anna." Dillon said grasping her delicate hand. "I guess Danny filled you in on our conversation yesterday?"

"He did. But we've got a lot to do today. How long do you think the tryout will last?"

"No more than an hour. Will that work?"

"*Yes,*" Danny interjected, before his mother could respond.

Reynolds looked to Anna, who nodded slightly.

"Okay, let's get started then."

He led the pair into the training facility towards the line of batting cages at the rear of the massive room.

"This is where we'll set up today," said Reynolds. "I brought in a couple of other players to help out. You can warm up with Juan." He gestured to a stocky Puerto Rican boy wearing shin guards and a chest protector.

"Take as much time as you need. I'm going to grab the Director so he can see you pitch. Anna, you're welcome to watch from here. Would you like me to grab you a chair?"

"I'm fine standing," she replied, pausing a moment before adding, "But thank you."

Reynolds couldn't help but notice how attractive she was. Instead of her typical ponytail, she wore her hair down today, the long locks flowing in dark waves over her shoulders. Reynolds wondered how old she was. She couldn't have been more than thirty. The thought reminded him that Danny had never mentioned his father. Looking at her hand there was no wedding ring.

*Interesting.* But there would be time for all that later. If the tryout went well, he hoped he'd be seeing a lot more of Danny *and* his mother.

The catcher approached Danny and stuck out a pudgy hand. "I'm Juan," he said.

"Danny."

"Good luck today," Juan said as the boys parted the netting and entered the cage.

"Thanks." Danny replied, butterflies churning in his stomach.

The cages were impressive. Inside the netting was a large dirt colored mat painted with a home plate and two batter's boxes. A rolling cart to the side held dozens of pristine white Rawlings baseballs inscribed with the words *Official Major League Baseball* and bearing the signature of Commissioner Rob Manfred.

Danny picked up one of the balls. He'd never held a brand-new baseball before. It felt smooth and perfect—much different from the scuffed and stained baseballs he was used to.

A large pitcher's mound covered in thick green synthetic turf sat toward the rear of the cage. As Danny approached the mound, Juan called out, "Let's warm up a little before you take the hill."

As the boys played catch Danny could feel his nerves dissipating. He began to realize that throwing a baseball here in this fancy place was no different from the dirt lot at home. It relaxed him, and he began stepping up the velocity of his throws.

A few moments later Reynolds returned to the cages, an older man in tow.

"Danny, I want you to meet Ed Hernandez," Dillon said, gesturing to the older man. "He's the Director of the Academy."

"Hello Danny," Hernandez bellowed. "I've heard a lot about you."

"Thank you, sir," Danny replied. "I really appreciate the tryout."

"Of course," Hernandez said. "You ready to get to work?"

Danny nodded and took the mound. He placed the edge

of his worn Nike against the thick piece of rubber at the rear of the mound and began his windup. His hands came together in front of him as he lifted his right leg, then took a huge stride down the mound and released a fastball.

The pitch thundered into the catcher's glove—waist high in the center of the plate. The *pop* of the pitch striking the glove echoed off the facility walls.

Hernandez turned to Reynolds, eyebrows raised and said quietly, "Not bad."

"Wait 'till you see his curve," Reynolds whispered back, not wanting to interrupt the pitcher's concentration.

Danny threw a few more fastballs, each one popping into the catcher's glove like the first.

Reynolds called out through the netting: "Let's see a breaking ball, Danny."

The boy nodded, adjusting his grip on the baseball. Again, he wound up and strode down the mound, releasing the ball this time with a flick of his wrist. The pitch started high, then broke sharply downward toward the plate.

It was poetry in motion. Hernandez was still skeptical, but was unexpectedly warming to the boy's talent. "Let's see what he can do against a hitter or two."

It seemed word of the new kid had spread quickly through the facility. Now a handful of the boys stood around the batting cage watching the tryout.

"Anyone want some extra BP today?" Reynolds said to the group.

Every hand shot up—each boy wanting to put the new kid in his place.

"Tomas," Reynolds said, pointing to a tall skinny boy from Mexico City. "Jump in there."

With Tomas settled in the batter's box, Danny began his windup then hurled the ball to the plate. Tomas took a mighty swing but came up empty as the pitch landed low and away.

Tomas fouled the next two pitches behind him and into the netting.

Three straight fastballs. *Time for a changeup,* Danny thought.

He gripped the ball in his palm and formed a circle with his index finger and thumb. Tomas, expecting another fastball, again swung for the fences. Again, he missed, his swing far too early as the ball landed safely in the catcher's glove.

"What do you think Ed?" Reynolds asked, a broad smile across his lips.

"I think the bet was that he could strike out Avila," Hernandez replied.

"Alright, alright," Reynolds said. "Alejandro!"

The boy stepped towards him. His slight build camouflaged the fact that he was the best contact hitter in the Academy.

"Let's see what you've got," Reynolds said as Avila entered the cage.

Danny's first pitch came in high and inside. Avila turned on the pitch, his compact swing ripping the ball foul to his left.

The next pitch was a ball, again high and inside. Danny adjusted his grip. It was time for something low and away.

Avila was not only athletic—he was also smart. He too anticipated the pitcher would come with something low and away. The pitch came in fast and farther outside than he'd expected. Avila threw his bat at the ball and barely made contact, the tip of his bat sending the ball into the netting on the side of the cage.

*One more strike*, Danny thought, mulling his next pitch.

Reynolds looked at Danny, anticipating he'd bring that wicked curveball. Avila was guessing the same. He would sit back in the box and wait on the curveball to hang, then crush it into the netting at the back of the cage.

But Danny wanted to make an impression. If Avila was their best, he wanted to challenge him and that meant one thing—fastball.

As Avila dug in, Danny wound up and pushed hard off the rubber. His long stride seemed to end halfway to home plate as he released the pitch, grunting with effort.

Waiting on the curveball, Avila didn't even have time to swing. Once he realized the pitch was a fastball, it was far too late. The ball landed squarely, with that sharp *pop* in the catcher's glove—waist high in the center of the plate.

Another strikeout.

The boys surrounding the cage laughed and howled at Avila. Reynolds couldn't understand most of what they were saying, but he could tell Alejandro wouldn't be living this moment down for a while.

Slowly, Ed Hernandez, reached in his pocket and produced a folded fifty-dollar bill. "A bet's a bet, amigo," he said to Reynolds, and handed him the bill.

"Well, what do you think?" Reynolds asked anxiously.

"You want to get his hat size, or should I?" Hernandez replied, the hint of a smile peeking out behind the handlebar mustache.

---

Aguado was rarely surprised. Living in the unpredictable world of the cartel had honed his criminal instincts to a razor-sharp edge. His trust was difficult, if not impossible, to earn. And his judge of character was usually impeccable.

But it appeared as if he'd misjudged Felix Martin. After their last meeting, he was certain he'd have to send Alvarez to Martin's lab to dispatch the chemist. Now he felt almost caught off guard. Martin had called two hours ago to say he'd cracked the code.

The formula was finally ready.

Still skeptical, Aguado had summoned Alvarez and Martin for another meeting in the study. Now the two men sat again on opposite ends of the grand sofa, facing Aguado as they had in the previous meeting.

"So, you've got it figured out?" Aguado asked, his voice tinged with suspicion.

"Right here, Jefe." Martin produced a small purple and gray thumb drive from his pocket and handed it over. "I brought a sample of the product as well."

As Martin handed over the small vials, Aguado eyed him cautiously. "And you've spoken to no one—not even the other chemists?"

"No one. As you know, I sent the other chemists away so I could concentrate, and I haven't talked to another soul since."

Aguado knew this was true. He'd allowed Martin to send the other chemists away, but the guards remained outside the lab. Martin hadn't left the building for days, and it showed on his weary face.

"I need a volunteer," Aguado said to no one in particular.

Both men looked up from the couch with the same expression. One that said, *I'm not trying that stuff.*

Before Aguado could ask again Alvarez rose from the sofa. "I'll go get someone."

He quickly returned with a young twentysomething man. The man was rail thin, and his shirt hung loosely off his shoulders. His eyes looked confused and terrified all at once as Alvarez explained what was needed of him.

Aguado popped the lids off each vial. "Tastes just like sugar?"

"Try it." Martin replied. "Completely harmless."

Aguado poured a small amount of the Azúcar into the palm of his hand. Wetting the tip of his pinky finger with this tongue, he stuck it into the pile, then put the finger to his lips.

Aguado's lips smacked as he tasted the product. "You've got the taste right. Now let's see if you managed the important part."

The words sent an unexpected surge of panic down Martin's spine. Suddenly, he realized he didn't know if the product really worked. Everything had looked good on paper, but he'd never actually tested it.

The chemist groaned and sank deeper into the sofa, wishing he could disappear into the thick down stuffing.

"You just mix the two?" Aguado asked.

"Yes, but you've got to get the dosage ..."

Aguado didn't take instruction from anyone, let alone the sniveling American chemist seated in front of him. He poured the remaining contents of the Azúcar into the vial of alcohol and watched as it dissolved in the liquid.

Their skinny test subject took a step backward, as if expecting the two substances to combust when combined—but nothing happened.

Aguado replaced the lid on the vial of alcohol and shook the solution, mixing the ingredients. He shoved the vial toward the skinny man and said, "Drink it."

The man cautiously reached for the vial and removed the cap. He said a silent prayer, then downed the vial as if it were a shot of tequila.

"It'll take some time to kick in," Martin said. "With a regular oral formula like Codeine it can take twenty to sixty minutes to feel the effects. I've modified Azúcar to hit the opiate receptors much faster. Should take between four and five minutes."

Aguado simply nodded.

The next five minutes would prove to be some of the longest of Martin's life. As they waited, he wondered what would happen to him if the drug didn't work. Beads of sweat began forming around his receding hairline, his pulse quickening with each passing second.

*It has to work,* he thought. *The science is undeniable.*

Breaking the deafening silence, Aguado asked the skinny man, "Anything?"

The man shook his head. "No, boss. I don't feel anythiii-innnng." His voice slurred slightly, and a child-like smile crept across his lips. "Notttthhhing ..." The man began giggling as the drug rushed through his system.

Suddenly his skin felt flushed and warm, and his feet were like steel anvils. The skinny man swallowed hard to wet his leathery throat, but couldn't work up any saliva. Instinctively he sat down before he lost his balance. His head rolled to the side and his eyes became glossy as he muttered incoherently under his breath.

"I think you've got your answer, Jefe," Alvarez said, watching the skinny man with a satisfied smile.

Aguado nodded his agreement. "Mr. Martin, you've done well."

Relief washed over Martin. "Thank you, Jefe."

Aguado turned his attention to Alvarez. "Mr. Martin just became the most valuable chemist in the world."

Alvarez smirked. "Yes, Jefe."

"Mr. Martin," Aguado continued. "We need to scale manufacturing immediately. You have all my resources at your disposal. Let me know what you need, and you shall have it."

## CHAPTER 6

The tryout couldn't have gone any better. Reynolds smiled broadly as he approached Danny, his mother by his side.

"I'd say that went pretty well." Reynolds patted Danny on the back. "I like how you went with the fastball on your last pitch—shows guts."

Danny grinned sheepishly, his eyes avoiding Reynolds'. "Probably just got lucky."

Reynolds shook his head. "Danny, in my experience, the harder you work, the luckier you get. Do you understand what that means?"

Danny shrugged his shoulders. "I think so."

Reynolds continued. "It means, if you want to train at the Academy, you're going to have to put in a lot of work. Hard work."

In unison, Danny and his mother froze and looked at Reynolds, eyes wide.

"You mean I'm in?" Danny was barely able to squeeze the words from his mouth.

"Yeah, you're in," Reynolds replied, thoroughly enjoying

the exchange. "You just struck out our best hitter. Alejandro doesn't strike out—ever."

"But Mr. Reynolds ..." Anna replied in a soft but firm voice. "We don't have the money for this. We appreciate the ..."

Reynolds immediately cut over her. "Oh, no need to worry about that. Some of the boys pay to train here, but for kids with Danny's talent level we accept the players on a speculative contract. Danny can live here, train here, and go to school here at no charge."

"And what's the catch?" Anna said, eyeing Reynolds suspiciously.

"It's not a catch as much as an investment." Reynolds explained. "The Academy and Danny will sign a contract guaranteeing his enrollment here at the Academy until he graduates. In exchange, we ask for the exclusive right to represent Danny when and if he signs his first contract."

"And if Danny decides not to play baseball after he graduates?" Anna pressed.

"Then we don't recoup our investment and Danny will have the benefit of a top-notch education for nothing."

Anna looked at Danny, his eyes shone with youthful energy and hope, two things that she'd let slip away over the years. If this was his chance to escape Villa Unión and build a better life, she knew she couldn't stand in the way.

"And he can come home on the weekends?" Anna asked, watching as the expression on Danny's face turned from apprehension to elation.

"Yes, unless we're traveling, he can be home every weekend if you'd like."

Anna exhaled as Danny wrapped his arms tightly around his mother and whispered, "Thanks mom. I'm going to make you proud."

"I know you will, Mijo," she said back. "I know you will."

Over the weeks that followed, Danny became something of a celebrity at the Academy. The other boys warmed to him quickly after his performance at the tryout, and his play continued to dazzle both teammates and coaches alike.

He was immediately the most dominant pitcher at the Academy, and his hitting was coming along nicely as well. His bat speed had improved dramatically since the tryout and his power seemed to increase daily, aided by the Academy's state-of-the-art weight room and high protein meal plans.

Reynolds had spent hours in the batting cages with Danny, tweaking and tuning his swing to perfection. And in doing so, the two had formed something of a bond. Danny would soak up as much baseball knowledge as Reynolds could provide, and in turn, Danny would help Reynolds with his Spanish. It was an easy friendship from the start.

Now, watching through the nylon netting of the batting cage, Reynolds and Ed Hernandez admired their young protégé with pride.

"I want to put him in front of the scouts in December," Hernandez said, gaze fixed on Danny.

"You really think he's ready?" Reynolds replied coyly, thinking it was about time Hernandez broached the subject.

"When you've been doing this as long as I have, you know when a kid is ready—and Danny's ready."

"Alright, alright, alright," Reynolds drawled in his best Matthew McConaughey impression, then flashed Hernandez his trademark smile.

---

Seated in his lab with two armed guards stationed at the entrance, Martin exhaled long and slow—a sigh of relief for the ages. Now all he had to do was put together a list of equipment and raw materials for the manufacturing facility. Piece of cake.

But as he pondered his next steps, Aguado's words crept into Martin's head like a harbinger of doom: *Mr. Martin just became the most valuable chemist in the world.*

Maybe it wasn't even the words so much as the look in his eye when Aguado spoke them. Martin knew Aguado was a dangerous and violent man, but he'd done a good job— been true to his word. Surely Aguado would agree.

In the back of his mind, however, Martin knew Aguado couldn't be trusted. There were only two men on earth that had a copy of the formula for Azúcar, and that made Martin a loose end.

The more he mulled over the scenario in his mind, the more his pulse raced. His palms began to sweat, and he swallowed hard, trying to soothe the lump in his throat. He didn't have any leverage. The formula had been his ace in the hole, and he'd handed it over on a silver platter.

Martin cursed himself for being so stupid and naïve. He'd been under so much pressure to complete the formula that he hadn't even bothered thinking of anything beyond that.

Sure, the cartel needed him to piece together a manufacturing facility. But then what? After that, Martin would essentially be dead weight—a walking liability.

He needed a backup plan—and fast. If Aguado was planning on killing him, he had to have an insurance policy.

But it wasn't like he could just call someone for help. Aguado had confiscated Martin's phone upon his arrival and there was no landline in the lab. He could try to email someone, but he knew his communications were being monitored. He'd be dead the second he hit *Send*.

Gazing blankly around the lab, searching for a plan, he

noticed a thumb drive atop his desk. It was identical to the one he'd given Aguado—purple with gray accents.

The drive gave him an idea. It was extremely risky, but at the moment Martin didn't have many other options.

He quickly opened a browser on his computer and searched for the nearest shipping center. Perfect—one of those mailbox stores was a five-minute walk from the lab. He would copy the formula to the drive, then write a letter detailing Aguado's operation and the key players in his entourage. He'd put both in a manilla envelope and give it to the shipping store with instructions to mail the envelope if he didn't return within thirty days. If Aguado tried anything funny, Martin would inform him the envelope would be mailed directly to the DEA.

It was a decent plan, and the more Martin mulled it over in his head, the more comfortable he became with the idea.

His hands were shaking now as he reached for the drive and inserted it into the USB port on his computer. Guiding the mouse slowly, he clicked the file containing the formula and dragged it to the thumb drive icon. The entire process took less than thirty seconds.

Martin removed the drive and held it up to his face. This ten-dollar piece of plastic and metal was the only thing standing between him and the full might of the most powerful cartel in Mexico.

Quickly, he shoved it in his pocket and began penning the letter.

## CHAPTER 7

December came before Reynolds could blink. This was the moment the boys, the coaches and everyone else at the Academy had been working towards for weeks. The scouts were scheduled to arrive at ten o'clock, and the building was buzzing with anticipation.

There were six scouts, each representing a different team: the Marlins, Astros, Twins, Reds, Yankees, and Dodgers. The scouts would observe for a couple of days and report back to their bosses which players they deemed to be true big-league prospects, worthy of a contract. And, of course, a hefty signing bonus.

It was against MLB rules to negotiate with a player until he turned sixteen years old, but Danny would be there soon enough. Even so, Reynolds had heard of clubs negotiating agreements with prospects as young as twelve.

The practice was technically against Major League rules, but since the agreements were mostly off the books, they were unenforceable, and the league mostly looked the other way.

That was the side of baseball Reynolds hated, the business side. He played for the love of the game, not for the money.

But then again, he had the luxury of growing up in a middle-class family, never rich but never wanting for anything. For many of these boys, baseball was a way out of poverty, for them and their families. Sure, they loved the game too, but the stakes were higher for them, and Danny was no different.

Reynolds approached Danny in the weight room. "You ready for today?"

The boy was busy stretching his left arm with a large elastic band clipped to a support beam.

"I think so," Danny replied nervously.

"Just act like they're not here." Reynolds instructed. "Just another day at the Academy."

Danny rolled his eyes. "Uh huh."

"Seriously. Don't let it get in your head. Shut everything out like you did at the tryout and you'll be fine. Trust me, you've got the talent Danny. Those scouts are going to be drooling over you after they see you pitch."

Danny could barely hear the words. His head was spinning as if in a dream. He was going to pitch in front of a scout from the Dodgers. The Los Angeles *Dodgers*!

"See you out there in ten," Reynolds said. He made sure to meet eyes with Danny. "You're going to do great."

"Thanks Dillon," Danny muttered, his mind obviously elsewhere.

The training facility was a hive of activity. Toward the far side of the room, two coaches set up lines of bright orange cones, as well as an electronic timer at each end to measure each boy's thirty-yard sprint time.

Across the room, another set of cones marked the CMJ station for Counter Movement Jumps. At this station, the player would complete three consecutive vertical jumps to measure repeated power and explosive movement.

In all, there were seven different stations. The boys

would be separated into numbered groups and move through each station throughout the day.

Ed Hernandez stood talking with a group of men Reynolds could only assume were the scouts. Catching his eye, Hernandez motioned for Reynolds to join them.

"Gentlemen, I'd like you to meet my understudy, Dillon Reynolds. Maybe one day I can convince him to run this place so I can retire on the beach."

The scouts grinned and introduced themselves one by one. The last man's name was James Duncan. He was stocky with a round face that was punctuated by a thick brown mustache. His crisp navy pullover read *Twins* across the chest.

Grabbing Reynolds' hand, Duncan said, "I remember that September you had with the Diamondbacks. Man, you were lights out. What'd you hit, seven, eight dingers in fourteen games?"

"Just six," Reynolds corrected with a smile. "Don't try to make me look better than I was."

Duncan chuckled. "That's what we do now, Dillon. When you're old like us, you sit around and talk about how great you used to be."

Another scout interjected, "Even if you were never that good," he said, pointing in Duncan's direction.

At this last part, all the men broke out in raucous laughter.

"Guess I'll have to work on that," Reynolds said.

"Gentlemen," Hernandez said. "Ready to get started?"

Each man nodded, and the group dispersed to watch the players complete various drills.

As James Duncan walked toward a neatly spaced row of synthetic pitching mounds, Reynolds caught up to him. He'd only just met the man, but he liked Duncan. He had kind eyes that mirrored his smile, and he moved with an understated confidence.

"Mr. Duncan?" Reynolds said.

"Call me James," Duncan replied.

"James. I've been working with a kid named Danny Rincon for the last few weeks. I think he has a chance to be something special."

Duncan's eyes narrowed. "Rincon." He mused to himself. "Don't think I know him."

"He's new to the Academy, and he hasn't been scouted before, so you probably wouldn't have him on your radar."

"Where'd he play before he came here?"

Reynolds paused. "Well ..."

Duncan raised his eyebrows.

"I found him playing street ball in Villa Unión. It's a town about thirty minutes from here."

Duncan's eyebrows rose even higher on his forehead. "*Street ball?*"

"I know it sounds crazy," Dillon continued. "But he can pitch, he can hit, and he's got a great mind for the game. He taught himself how to pitch from watching YouTube videos."

At this, Duncan let out an unexpected chortle. "YouTube you say?"

Reynolds held up his hands. "Just give him a look."

From a duffel bag at his feet, Duncan removed an iPad. "I'll make a note of him. Thanks for the heads up."

"You bet," Reynolds replied, before leaving Duncan and heading toward the center of the turf to the broad jump station.

The station consisted of two flat yellow and gray bars, running parallel to each other. Each bar contained a series of sensors to measure distance, flight time, jump power and other variables.

Reynolds would spend the day here, running the boys through a series of long jumps. The system would record their performance on a laptop and the data would be distributed to each scout electronically.

The day would be somewhat monotonous, Reynolds knew. Baseball had become so analytics-driven that scouts wanted every piece of data they could get their hands on. That meant measuring athleticism, speed, intelligence and a thousand other variables that make up a ball player.

But tomorrow would be different. Tomorrow the boys would hit, pitch and field in front of the scouts. Really get to show their God-given talents. That's when Reynolds knew Danny would shine.

---

Martin licked the gluey tab on the lip of the manilla envelope and pressed it shut, then added a piece of tape to the opening to make sure it was secure.

Everything was in place. The thumb drive containing the formula was sealed in the envelope along with the letter explaining Aguado's operation. He'd have to wait to address the envelope until he got to the mailbox store. There was no way he could chance someone walking into the lab and seeing an envelope addressed to the DEA.

Now came the hard part. Martin had to figure out how to slip out of the lab, deliver the envelope, then slip back in without being detected.

The lab was a nondescript white brick building, no more than two-thousand square feet. A white-painted door made of vertical pine slats marked the entrance, flanked by a pair of bar clad windows that had been covered from the inside with cardboard.

In addition to the workspace, the lab contained a

makeshift living quarters, complete with bedroom, bathroom, and a tiny kitchenette, specifically built so Martin would rarely have to leave the building.

As he looked around the room, Martin's eyes searched for a plan. The front door and windows were obviously not an option, since the guards were stationed there twenty-four seven. The door in the back was blocked from the outside by a wall of rusted fifty-gallon drums—way too noisy to move. And the side windows were all barred shut.

"Think." Martin's voice echoed inside the small space. He tilted his head back and ran a hand through what was left of his thinning hair. Sighing, he returned his gaze to the room around him, then shot his eyes back up to the ceiling.

*"Bingo!"* There was a small hatch in the middle of the ceiling—most likely a roof access. He could stack a few crates on the floor, high enough to access the hatch then walk to the edge of the roof and lower himself down. Using the rear alley, he could make it to the mailbox store and back before anyone was the wiser.

Armed with a plan, Martin approached the Bluetooth speaker on his desk and pressed play. A stream of classical music flowed from the device, just loud enough to mask any noises stemming from his pending escape.

Tucking the manilla envelope into the back of his pants, Martin turned his attention to a stack of empty crates that had been used to ship the lab equipment. One by one, he stacked the wooden boxes into a pyramid and climbed to the top, studying the rectangular hatch.

Martin placed his fingertips on the wooden door and pressed upward. The hatch gave a bit but didn't open. Years of grime and grit had most likely coated the opening, essentially gluing it shut.

He pressed harder, and the hatch gave a bit more. Taking a deep breath, he pushed upward again, this time with all his might. A sharp *crack* rang through the lab as the door broke free of its frame, raining down bits of debris.

Martin froze. Had the guards heard? There was no way he could explain the stack of crates in the center of the room. *This could be a disaster!* he thought, holding his breath and waiting for the men to burst through the door.

But as the seconds ticked by, the door didn't open. And the men didn't burst in. There was just the soothing sound of Beethoven's Fifth wafting through the lab.

A bead of sweat rolled down Martin's cheek. He wiped it away, then gripped his hands around the frame of the access door. The roof joists creaked in protest as he heaved his body through the hole and onto the flat gravel rooftop. Again, he waited. Again, no activity below.

Martin crept to the edge of the roof; its eaves overhanging the wall by a good two feet. He could grab on to the edge of the eave and hang his legs over, then simply drop the remaining couple of feet to the ground.

One by one Martin swung his legs over the edge, the front of his khaki pants scraping across the tar and gravel. With his entire body now hanging from the roofline, he released his grip.

The next few seconds moved in hyper slow motion. As his body descended to the ground, Martin's leg caught on something. His right knee twisted and buckled inward, causing him to fall to the ground in a tangled heap. The noise was deafening—at least in Martin's ears.

As he attempted to recover, he gazed down, his leg had become intertwined with the frame of an abandoned ten-speed bicycle that had been leaning against the outside wall of the lab. The eaves had concealed the bike on his initial survey, and he'd landed directly on top of it.

*Why now?* his brain screamed.

As he rose, he heard footsteps, crunching near the front

of the building. Panic racked him, adrenaline rising toward fight or flight. Not being much of a fighter, he chose flight and swung his battered leg over the bike.

"Hey!" the voice called behind him. "What the hell's going on?"

———

Reynolds was correct. The previous day had been a monotonous routine, recording long jump after long jump for the better part of six hours. But the measurements were complete, and the scouts had their data to analyze.

Now came the fun part.

The boys gathered around Ed Hernandez in the center of the training facility while the scouts stood outside the circle, sipping paper cups of coffee from the cafeteria.

"Today we're going to run through some live action drills," said Hernandez. "Most of you will be working in the batting cages with Coach Reynolds this morning. If you're a pitcher, you'll be with me by the mounds. Any questions?"

The boys each shook their heads and began splitting into groups, with the majority heading towards the batting cages. Reynolds wished he could be with the pitchers to see Danny throw but that wasn't his area of expertise and Ed needed help with the hitters today.

Before Danny could make his way to the pitchers' workout, Reynolds pulled him aside. "Today's your time to shine, Danny."

The boy looked back at Reynolds, a grimace on his face.

"What's wrong?" Reynolds asked.

"I don't know," Danny replied softly. "Nerves I guess."

Reynolds grabbed Danny by both shoulders and squeezed, his voice becoming businesslike. "I believe in you

Danny. You wouldn't be here if you weren't good. Now go out there today and show it—just like in the tryout."

Trying to break the tension, Reynolds continued, "Because if you don't, I'm going to kick your ass."

Danny grinned and nodded, then headed toward the line of pitchers' mounds at the far end of the facility.

As he headed in the opposite direction, Reynolds felt a tug on his arm. He turned to see James Duncan, the scout from the Twins.

"Hey James, how's it going?"

"Good, Dillon. I got a look at your boy Danny yesterday."

"What did you think?"

"His measurables are all in line. He's got a couple areas to work on, but nothing that can't be taught."

"That's great news," Reynolds replied. "But today is where you'll see him shine. Danny can really throw."

"You really like this kid, don't you?"

"I do, James. He hasn't had it easy. Single mother. Dirt poor ..." His voice trailed off. "But he's never complained about it once. He's a hard worker and a good kid."

Duncan stared back, a fatherly smile donning his face. "You can't teach that stuff, Dillon. We need more of that in baseball. Nowadays, it's all contracts and endorsements. Me, me, me."

Reynolds nodded. He'd been there once, and he knew how it worked. It was easy for a young man to get caught up in the glitz and glam.

"Couldn't agree more," Reynolds said, giving Duncan a knowing look.

Turning toward the pitching mounds, Duncan said, "I'll find you later and let you know how it goes with Danny today."

Reynolds thanked him and continued forward to the

group of anxious hitters milling about near the batting cages.

As the boys warmed up, playing catch behind the mounds, James Duncan scanned the tablet in his hand. He scrolled up and down through the columns of stats and measurements, finally landing on Danny Rincon.

He thought about the conversation with Reynolds. How glowingly he spoke about the boy. Of course, Duncan had heard glowing reviews of thousands if not tens of thousands of other prospects. Some worked out—most didn't. But still, something in the way Reynolds talked about Danny was different.

He highlighted Danny's name, as he'd done with a handful of other prospects he'd be watching closely today. If things went well, he'd give his recommendation to the Twins' management team, and they'd have a few more talented prospects to add to their pipeline.

Meanwhile, Danny removed the black A.B.S. pullover and set it aside, stretching his left arm across his chest.

He breathed in deeply, trying to calm the butterflies. Four of the six scouts were currently watching the pitchers, and Danny eyed them curiously as they fiddled about with charts and notebooks, wondering what was written on the pages.

Then, from the last of the three pitching mounds, Hernandez shouted, "Rincon, you're up."

Danny grabbed his glove and hustled toward him. Heart pounding, he climbed atop the synthetic turf and braced his left foot against the pitching rubber.

"Throw a few warmup pitches, Danny, then we'll get to work," Hernandez instructed.

He threw a dozen or so practice pitches, but still didn't feel comfortable on the mound. He always got nervous taking the hill, but the jitters usually left once he started throwing.

"Alright Danny, let's get into it," Hernandez called.

Danny closed his eyes for a moment, breathing in short gasps. He went into his windup slower than usual, trying to ensure the first pitch was perfect. The urge to guide the ball into the catcher's glove overtook him, and, inadvertently, he changed his release.

The deviation proved a huge mistake. Instead of guiding the ball into the catcher's glove, Danny's release was late, sending the ball bouncing in front of the plate and spinning away into the netting.

He watched as two of the scouts exchanged silent glances.

Danny's hands began to tremble. This was his worst nightmare. There were four major league scouts here watching him. They'd flown hundreds, maybe thousands of miles to see him and he was blowing it.

He punched his glove and grabbed a new ball from the cart at his side. He felt the seams and turned the ball over in his hand, placing his index and ring finger vertically along the red stitching.

*A simple two seam fastball,* he thought. *Easy.*

Again, he wound up and fired the ball at the catcher, this time overcorrecting and releasing his grip too early. The pitch sailed over the catcher's outstretched glove and slid down the back wall of the cage, landing softly in a pile of netting on the floor.

This time, he could hear the scouts mumbling to each other.

He rubbed his eyes, inwardly cursing himself for choking under pressure.

As the scouts continued to mumble, a voice called out: "Danny."

It was the scout from the Twins. He parted the nylon netting of the cage and motioned Danny to a corner. "Nervous up there?"

Danny's tongue was thick, and his throat was dry. He wanted to speak, but all he could do was nod and look down at the turf.

"Tell me this, Danny. What's the worst thing that can happen today?"

Danny looked back, confused. He paused for a moment to think and said, "I blow the tryout."

Duncan nodded. "Yeah, that would be bad." Then the pitch in his voice rose slightly. "But would you still have a roof over your head and a hot meal to eat tonight?"

Puzzled, Danny replied cautiously, "Yeah."

"Would your mom still love you?" Duncan pressed.

Danny nodded. "Yeah."

"Would your arm fall off?"

Danny laughed at this. "No." he said, grinning.

"So, what you're telling me is your life wouldn't be over, right?"

Duncan could see the wheels turning in Danny's head and continued. "It's okay to have nerves. That means you care. I want you to get back on the mound and take three deep breaths before your windup. Then throw like you always do. Don't adjust your technique because we're here."

The scout smiled and patted Danny on the shoulder, then stepped back out of the cage.

As he returned to the mound, Danny repeated the mantra in his head: *What's the worst thing that could happen?* He repeated the words over and over.

Suddenly, it dawned on him—the worst thing that could happen, *had* happened. Two bad pitches. Horrible pitches. But he still had a chance. And the scout was right. If he failed today, he would be no worse off than when he was playing ball in the streets of Villa Unión.

Danny stared into the catcher's glove and took three deep breaths. The breathing seemed to give him tunnel vision as he began his windup. Kicking up a knee, Danny pulled his arm back and fired a fastball. It landed with a loud *snap* in the catcher's glove—waist high and over the plate.

He looked back at the Twins scout and the man returned his stare with a knowing wink and a paternal smile.

A few pitches in and the nerves were gone. Danny hurled fastballs, curveballs, and off-speed pitches—each one perfectly centered over the target.

Now, instead of low murmurs, the scouts furiously scribbled notes and shot video from their cell phones. Within minutes, the two remaining scouts made their way from the batting cages to the mounds to watch Danny throw.

With each pitch, Danny's confidence grew, and his nerves receded. He could feel the familiar ease returning to his motion. His fastball became harder and heavier. His curveball broke more sharply, and his changeup seemed to float into the catcher's glove.

The scouts buzzed amongst each other.

Hernandez looked towards them. "Seen enough, gentlemen?"

Each man nodded, and Hernandez turned his attention to Danny. "Alright Danny, good job today."

"Thanks coach," Danny replied and exited the cage, head still spinning.

With his pitching session complete, Danny began making his way toward the batting cages. As he walked by the first cage, he caught Reynolds' eye.

Reynolds held out his hands, palms up, silently saying, "How'd it go?"

Danny replied simply by pumping his fist twice and smiling ear to ear.

---

That evening, Reynolds sat across from Hernandez in a large modern corner office. The L-shaped desk was made of thick glass and chrome, with a laptop computer perched on its surface. The wall behind Hernandez was adorned with various awards and photographs from his playing career, while the opposite wall held a sixty-inch flat screen television playing a rerun of the 1989 American League Championship series—Oakland vs. Boston.

"How do you think it went today?" Reynolds asked.

"Not bad. I think a couple of the boys will get offers by the end of the week."

"How'd Danny do?"

"He started rough, but James Duncan talked to him and settled him down. After that, he was lights out. I thought a couple of the scouts were going to offer him on the spot."

Reynolds knew he liked Duncan.

"Good," Reynolds said. "I didn't get a chance to talk to him after the pitching session."

A knock came from the door and Hernandez called out to his visitor. "James, c'mon in. Have a seat."

James Duncan took the chair next to Reynolds. "Hope I'm not interrupting anything."

"Not at all," Hernandez assured him. "We were just talking about Danny Rincon."

Duncan answered back. "*Everyone* is talking about Danny Rincon. I'm afraid the Twins are going to have some competition for him."

Hernandez rose an eyebrow. "You think so?"

"I know so," Duncan answered flatly. "I already heard

from our GM back in Minneapolis—rumor is the Astros want him bad."

Hernandez smiled at this. He knew the more competition for Danny, the higher the signing bonus. "Well, James, we just want Danny to land with the right organization. Somewhere he can continue to develop."

"You've seen our farm system, Ed. You know we've got some of the best developmental coaches in the league." Duncan said, hoping to strengthen his case.

"We have full confidence in the Twins organization James. When do you think you'll have something for us to look at?"

"I'd bet as soon as Thursday, maybe Friday, at the latest."

"That sounds great." Hernandez said. "And if you need anything in the meantime, we're at your disposal."

Duncan rose and offered a hand to Hernandez, then Reynolds. "Thank you both, especially you." He said to Reynolds as he left the office.

"What was that all about?" Hernandez asked.

"I might've given Danny a little plug yesterday. I like James, seems like a straight shooter. If the Twins are anything like he is, Danny will be in a great situation."

"I agree." Hernandez replied. "I've known James for many years. What you see is what you get."

Reynolds nodded, rising from his chair. "Going to be a long couple of days until Thursday."

Hernandez smirked. "For you or for Danny?"

# CHAPTER 8

It was indeed a long couple of days. After the scouts left, the Academy returned to business as usual, and the boys went back to their normal routine.

But Thursday had come and gone, with no offer from the Twins or the Astros.

Hernandez had assured Reynolds to be patient, that the wheels of Major League Baseball turn slowly at times—a task that had proved difficult. Especially with Danny pestering him multiple times a day to see if an offer had come in, each time being disappointed with the answer.

It was now Friday, and as Reynolds crossed the turf of the training facility, Hernandez blocked his path. "Got a minute?"

"Sure."

Hernandez lowered his voice. "Three offers came in for Danny this morning. The Astros, the Twins, and the Reds."

A surge of adrenaline coursed through Reynolds' veins —almost as if *he* had been offered the contracts. "Three? That's great news!" He lowered his voice. "What kind of numbers are we looking at?"

"I want you to find out when Danny finds out."

Reynolds looked puzzled as Hernandez continued. "I wondered if you wanted to present the offers to Danny and his mother?" He smiled. "He's your boy after all."

He could see the look of excitement on Reynolds' face, and continued, "Of course, I'll need to handle the actual negotiations, but this could be a fun first step for you. Make it ceremonial. Take them to dinner, courtesy of the Academy."

Reynolds beamed. "Ed, that's awesome. I'd love to present the offers."

"Then it's settled," Hernandez replied. "Swing by my office when you have a minute. I'll have copies of the paperwork ready for you."

An extra spring in his step, Reynolds strode through the training facility. This would prove to be a red-letter day for Danny and his mother.

Reynolds couldn't wait to tell them the good news. As he approached the field outside, where the Friday scrimmage was about to start, he spotted Danny warming up in the bullpen.

A half wall lined with green padding separated the bullpen from the field. Two sets of pitchers and catchers warmed up while the coaches sorted out their lineups.

"Danny," Reynolds called, motioning for the boy to come over.

As Danny approached, Reynolds felt as though the news might explode from his chest instead of his mouth. A sly grin immediately crept over his face. Calming his voice, he whispered so the other boys wouldn't hear.

"The offers came in this morning."

Danny's eyes widened. "The Astros and Twins?"

"Don't forget about the Reds."

"The Reds too?" Danny pumped his fist in excitement. "Did they say how much?"

"I haven't seen the numbers yet. But I spoke to Ed this afternoon, and he wants me to present the offers to you and your mom."

"When?"

"Maybe next week," Reynolds replied coyly, knowing Danny could never wait that long.

He saw the look of protest wash over Danny's face and backpedaled. "I'm kidding. I know you can't wait that long. How about tonight, five o'clock? We can meet in the lobby, then go to dinner in town."

"Awesome!" Danny replied. "I'll call my mom after the scrimmage."

"Perfect." He gave Danny a fist bump and headed back to the training facility.

As Reynolds walked, he thought back to the night he'd signed his first contract. The signing bonus had seemed absurdly large at the time—even his parents were shocked at the amount.

They'd sat around the kitchen table with the Diamondback's scout and Assistant GM and made them go through the document line by line, per his father's request. It took a couple of hours to read every word and by the end, Reynolds' head was spinning. He'd understood less than half of the language in the contract, but his dad was smart, and he knew he could rely on him to interpret all the legal mumbo jumbo.

Reynolds wondered how Danny would feel without a father there to guide him. Would he feel the same confidence in his mother? Would his mother understand the contract? Hell, would Reynolds understand the contract? He'd only seen a handful of them over his twenty-six years, and they all seemed like they were written in a foreign language.

Ed would be a good asset to Danny and his mother,

though. If the Rincons had questions, Ed most likely had the answers.

Reynolds decided that tonight would be informal, more of a celebration than a meeting. They'd look over the offers, have a good meal, and allow Danny to simply soak in the moment.

---

Martin knew the men wouldn't shoot him. He was too valuable—at least for now. But his plan to slip out of the lab undetected was ruined. He had to escape, and he had to do it now. If the guards caught him with the envelope, he would surely be killed. At this point, he'd probably be killed even without the envelope.

Martin curled an arm around his back and felt for the package. It was still there. Good. He might need it for leverage, if he could manage to escape his current predicament.

Before the guards knew what was happening, Martin pushed off hard against the dirt road and launched the rusty bike down the narrow alleyway behind the lab.

The men began screaming at each other and chasing him, but with the aid of the bike, Martin was much faster and began to disappear down the alley.

Realizing this, the men rushed to a Toyota pickup truck parked in front of the lab. The driver started the engine, shoved the gearshift into first and lurched the vehicle forward. The truck slowly gained speed and careened around the corner, then took a hard left down the alleyway where Martin had fled.

Amid the chaos, the men could still make out the chemist pedaling furiously down the narrow backstreet, approaching a busy intersection.

As the truck gained ground, the bike disappeared

around a sharp corner onto a four-lane avenue. Small shops and restaurants lined the roadway and at just after five o'clock in the afternoon, the area was flooded with cars and pedestrians.

Looking back, Martin could see the truck was hemmed in by a line of traffic blocking the intersection. Hopefully, the guards would get stuck in the snarl of cars, and he could disappear amongst the throngs of people.

As the truck stopped before the line of traffic, the driver laid on the horn as his passenger pointed a pistol out the window, waving at a terrified cab driver to back up. Message received: the cabbie threw the vehicle into reverse and sent the taxi pitching back a few feet, its bumper crunching into an idling concrete truck behind it.

The Toyota pounced on the opening and shot through the narrow gap. The vehicle bounced over a yellow painted curb and onto the sidewalk. Pedestrians leapt out of the truck's path as it steered around the traffic and back onto the street, speeding toward Martin.

He pedaled faster now, the bicycle weaving erratically through the busy street. Martin was breathing heavy, sucking in huge gulps of smoggy air into his tired lungs. He knew he couldn't keep this up for long.

Hoping he'd lost the guards, Martin turned to see if the truck was still in pursuit. To his horror, the truck had made it through the traffic and was now behind him on the avenue. The driver wove wildly through traffic, veering from one side of the road to the other and closing in fast.

As Martin returned his gaze to the traffic ahead, he shrieked in horror. In front of him, a massive delivery van was oncoming, mere feet away. The driver waved frantically and honked for him to get out of the way.

Martin jerked the bike off the Avenue, barely avoiding a head-on collision with the grill of the van. But in his panic, he missed the cement curb marking the side of the roadway. The impact of the tire hitting the concrete edge launched Martin up and over the handlebars of the bike.

His body hurtled through the air, head over heels, in the warm Mexican afternoon. The curb ran parallel to a small street cafe and Martin's body sailed into the patio area, colliding with a stunned group of diners. Refried beans and bowls of salsa exploded into the air as his body slammed into the table and sent searing pain through his side and down his leg. His head smashed into the metal edge of the table and a trickle of crimson now streamed down his temple.

A woman in the corner screamed and the other diners looked on in disbelief at the chaotic scene unfolding in front of them.

Martin was dazed, feeling ironically like he'd been hit by a truck. He was seeing double now, no doubt from the blow to the head. As he stared up at the sky, the world began to fade slowly into darkness.

"You ok, buddy?"

The voice snapped him back to the present, and bright light began to replace the darkness. A young man stood over him, looking concerned.

Martin strained to refocus his vision until finally there was one man above him instead of two.

"I'm, I'm fine," he stammered, attempting to stand.

A small crowd had begun to form, and the man put a hand on his shoulder. "Maybe you shouldn't get up just yet."

Martin brushed the man's hand away and rose to his feet on wobbly legs. As he attempted to steady himself, Martin heard a vehicle skid to a halt in front of the cafe and turned to see his pursuers exiting the Toyota pickup.

*Shit!* He had to go now.

At some point during the collision, the manilla envelope

containing the drive must have dislodged itself from the back of his pants. But now, instead of one envelope there were two, and he didn't have time to grab the one that rested on the patio behind the overturned table.

Hoping for a stroke of good luck, Martin grabbed the envelope nearest him and bolted down the street in a panic, leaving the rusty bike intertwined with the metal table. The two men from the truck gave chase on foot, following Martin down an alleyway a short distance from the cafe.

The alley was narrow, filled with trash and piles of construction debris. Martin could hear the men getting closer. His lungs began burning again, adding to the pain in his head and his side. He needed an exit and he needed it now.

Up ahead, he spotted a vine covered chain-link fence at the end of the alley. It stood guard over a vacant lot strewn with discarded chunks of concrete between the dense patches of overgrowth.

Maybe he could conceal himself among the vegetation —it was the only plan he could come up with. Close to the fence now, he flung himself onto the wire mesh, hands stinging as the sharp edges of the galvanized steel dug into his palms. Jamming the toe of his shoe into an opening in the chain link, Martin heaved himself upward.

But as he began to lift his leg over the fence, a pair of hands grasped his ankle and pulled downward. He held on to the top of the fence with a death-grip and flailed about, trying to break the iron grip, but another pair of hands clamped around his other ankle and pulled viciously, tearing him off the fence and onto the ground.

Martin landed in a heap, and his head bounced off a rock protruding from the hard packed dirt. It was the second time in less than ten minutes he'd sustained a significant blow to the head and this time it proved too much. He turned and looked up at the cloudless evening sky. The world began to dim, the lights slowly fading.

———

The Academy's executive offices were nearly empty on a Friday afternoon. Most of the staff had left early to get a head start on the weekend.

As Reynolds traversed the maze of cubicles planted in the center of the floor, he could see Ed Hernandez was still in his office.

Hernandez had a cell phone to his ear, but he motioned for Reynolds to come in. "Yes, I know the interest is high, but you'll easily be able to pay it all back when Alejandro gets his signing bonus." Hernandez paused, listening, then continued. "Okay, talk it over. You know where to reach me."

He ended the call and set the phone down on the glass top desk. "Work is never done." He sighed. "You here to get the offers for Danny?"

"Sure am," Reynolds replied.

Hernandez stood up, approached a tall black filing cabinet in the corner of the office and removed a large manilla envelope from the top drawer.

"Here they are. The Twins, Astros, and Reds." Hernandez handed the envelope across the desk. "We'll want to negotiate with the clubs for a higher number, but I'm pleasantly surprised at the initial offers."

Reynolds took the envelope and smiled. "This is going to be life changing for Danny and his mom. It's just hard to believe how all this worked out."

"Just goes to show you—if you've got talent, you'll get found sooner or later."

The phone on Hernandez's desk buzzed. "I've got to take this," he said. "Good luck tonight."

Reynolds walked to his small dorm room to drop off the envelope and headed back downstairs to watch the Friday afternoon scrimmage. The game was close, but in the bottom of the ninth inning Danny's team hit a walk-off double with a runner on first to win the game.

As Danny emerged from the dugout, bag over his shoulder, Reynolds called to him. "Danny, over here."

Danny seemed to bounce his way toward Reynolds, nervous energy bursting from his arms and legs. Removing a cell phone from his pocket, Reynolds asked, "You want to call your mom now?"

Danny smiled and nodded vigorously. He quickly took the phone and punched in the number.

"Hola mom," he said, the broad smile still plastered over his face. "Guess what?" He paused for a moment. "We got the offers!" Another pause as he listened. "Yeah, three of them. The Twins, the Astros, and the Reds. Dillon wants to present them to us tonight at dinner. Can you meet here in the lobby around five?"

Reynolds watched happily as the boy talked to his mother. This would be one of the best days of Danny's life—one he'd remember forever.

"Okay mom, see you then." Danny handed the phone back to Reynolds. "She'll meet us here at five."

"Sounds good." Reynolds replied. "I'm going to go shower before dinner. See you in the lobby."

Post shower, Reynolds headed to the lobby where Danny was already waiting, pacing a groove in the polished concrete floor.

"Ready to eat? I'm starving," Reynolds said, the manilla envelope in his hand.

For the first time in his life, Danny couldn't care less about food. His stomach was knotted with giddy anticipation about the offers.

He eyed the envelope. "Are those the offers?"

"Oh these? Nah, just some paperwork I forgot to drop off." Reynolds smiled impishly.

"C'mon Dillon."

"Alright, yes, these are the offers. All three of them."

The smile returned to Danny's face just in time to see his mother slow the rusty Corolla to a stop in front of the glass doors of the lobby. "That's her, let's go."

He was out the door in an instant, leaving Reynolds standing awkwardly alone in the lobby. "After you." Reynolds muttered and headed for the door.

Anna Rincon drove a 2003 Toyota Corolla that was nearing two-hundred-thousand miles. It was painted beige, but could also have been white that hadn't been washed in months, Reynolds couldn't quite tell. The front bumper was dented and missing large sections of paint. The hubcaps were missing, too, leaving behind plain black wheels wrapped in balding tires.

"Hola," Anna said as Reynolds stuffed his large frame into the back seat.

"Hola. Good to see you again, Anna."

"Good to see you too, Mr. Reynolds. Where are you taking us this evening?"

"You're in for a treat tonight." Reynolds replied. "There's a great little place off La Marina Avenue. It's called Bohemia Birrieria. Their carne asada is amazing."

"Yes, I know the place."

Reynolds could see Anna had come straight from work. She wore a powder blue uniform trimmed in white on the collar and sleeves with matching pants that hung loosely around her legs. A tight bun was knotted at the back of her head, and it bobbed up and down as the car bounced along the uneven road.

"Danny tells me he got three offers?" Anna asked from the front seat.

Reynolds could see her looking back at him in the rearview mirror, eyes silently assessing him.

"Yeah, we got offers from the Astros, the Twins and the Reds."

"Which one of those is closest to Mazatlán?" Anna asked.

"Definitely the Astros," Reynolds replied.

"Then that's the one I hope he chooses," she stated flatly, patting Danny on the knee.

"Unfortunately, it's a bit more complicated than that. You see, Danny will have to work his way through the minor leagues before he gets to the parent club—and that could land him in any number of places. He really won't be able to choose where he goes."

Danny's mother seemed to digest the information before speaking again. "I see."

Reynolds squirmed a bit in his seat, and was glad he'd chosen a restaurant close to the Academy. Anna Rincon was a tough nut to crack. No doubt about that.

The car slowed to a stop in front of the restaurant and the trio exited the vehicle. The smell of roasted meat and Mexican spices filled the air, sparking pangs of hunger in Reynolds' stomach.

It was a warm winter evening, and the group decided to sit on the patio that ran along the front of the building. The space was packed with tables full of diners busily eating, talking, laughing, and drinking.

Reynolds made small talk with Anna, saying something funny here and there, to which Anna would always return a polite smile but never laugh. He'd never encountered such an uphill climb before, when attempting to connect with the fairer sex. This was a first.

The sound of sizzling beef on a searing hot platter filled the patio, causing other diners to turn and stare at the dishes. The plates steamed and popped as the waiter lowered his tray and passed them, one by one, around the table.

"Bon Appetit." Reynolds stuck a fork into the seared cut of carne asada.

Anna looked back puzzled, clearly not understanding, but gave a polite smile anyway.

As Reynolds chewed a mouthful of the succulent steak, he spotted a man pedaling furiously down the street on a bicycle. There was a large delivery van headed straight for him, but the man's head was turned, looking backward. Reynolds cringed and wanted to cry out, but the food in his mouth wouldn't allow it.

The man jerked his head back around and saw the van just in time to veer off the road. His front tire smashed against the tall curb in front of the patio and catapulted the rider into the air. Anna's eyes went wide, and Danny's jaw dropped at the sight. The man was twisting and turning in the air, heading straight for their table.

Reynolds angled his bulk in front of Anna to block the man from hitting her and put an arm over his face.

The cyclist missed Reynolds but impacted the table squarely. His body skidded across the surface, sending food flying in every direction.

For a moment, the patio was blanketed in a stunned silence. Then a woman in the corner screamed. Reynolds looked at Anna and Danny, their shirts covered in globs of refried beans and wet patches of Coca-Cola.

"You guys okay?" he asked.

Each nodded in return, still too shocked to speak.

The man's mangled body lay in a crumpled pile on the other side of the small table. Gathering himself, Reynolds stood and approached the man, who was now moaning in pain. "You ok, buddy?"

The man seemed to ponder the question for a moment before replying slowly in a strained voice. "I'm ... I'm fine."

As the man attempted to regain his feet, Reynolds put a hand on his shoulder. "Maybe you shouldn't get up just yet."

But the man quickly brushed his hand away and rose, turning toward the street with a look of terror on his face.

During the commotion, a small white pickup truck had screeched to a halt in front of the restaurant. Two clearly agitated men emerged from the vehicle, each wielding a chrome plated pistol.

As Reynolds' attention was focused on the men from the truck, the cyclist snatched the manilla envelope from the wreckage of food and bolted down the sidewalk, the two men giving chase.

"Hey!" Reynolds shouted, but the trio continued down the street and turned down an alleyway, disappearing out of sight.

"What is it?" Danny asked.

"That guy just took the envelope with the offers," Reynolds said, still staring down the street.

He felt a tap on his shoulder and Reynolds turned his attention back to the table. Danny stood beside him, a smile on his face, manilla envelope in his hand.

*What envelope had the cyclist grabbed then?* Reynolds wondered, as two waiters hurried out of the restaurant, armed with mops and towels.

As they cleared the shattered plates and piles of cold food strewn across the patio, a chubby man in a dark suit and red tie appeared from inside the restaurant and offered his apologies.

Reynolds assured him they were fine, and the man promised to return shortly with a new set of entrees.

Now covered in a fresh tangerine-colored cloth and set with clean plates and glasses, the group reseated themselves at the table.

Reynolds looked at Anna, cleared his throat and deadpanned, "Well, I told you we were in for a treat tonight." A grin slowly crept over his face and the table burst out in laughter. It was the first time Reynolds had seen Anna produce a genuine smile.

*Worth the wait,* he thought, and grabbed the envelope.

"I think we better open this, don't you?"

Danny nodded his head.

Reynolds slid a finger under the lip of the envelope, tore open the top and pulled a sheet of paper from inside. It was handwritten in blue pen.

Reynolds scanned the page, bewildered. *What the hell is this?* he thought.

"Well?" Danny pressed.

Reynolds' face immediately straightened. "The offers aren't in here," he replied, and stuck his hand back inside the envelope. "I have no idea what this is, either."

He removed a small purple and gray thumb drive from the packet and set it on the table.

## CHAPTER 9

The lab was just as he left it. The pyramid of crates still stood neatly stacked in the center of the room. This time, however, instead of manning one of the many whirring machines or pounding away on his keyboard, Martin sat on a small rolling chair in the center of the room, hands zip-tied in front of him.

"Where were you going, Felix?" Aguado hissed.

Aguado and Alvarez stood over the seated Martin, their stares burning through him like white hot laser beams.

"I can explain." The words came out of Martin's mouth before he knew what he was saying, because he most definitely could not explain this away.

"I'm sure you can," Aguado said, holding up the food stained manilla envelope. "Why don't you start by explaining this?"

Martin's heart sank when he saw the package. Now, instead of an insurance policy, the envelope contained a death sentence. And once Aguado had confirmed Martin planned to rat him out to the DEA, the penalty would surely be death—and not a quick one.

He lowered his head and whispered, tears beginning to

stream down his face. "I'm sorry Jefe. I'm so sorry." Martin looked up at the men, salty rivulets staining his ruddy cheeks. "Please, I don't want to die! I'll do anything."

Aguado and Alvarez exchanged confused glances, puzzled by Martin's reaction. They'd seen what was inside the envelope already. It held a couple of baseball contracts, nothing more. Why was Martin reacting like this?

"Explain," Aguado demanded.

"I wasn't going to use it, Jefe. I just wanted an insurance policy in case you ..." His voice cracked and trailed off before continuing. "... didn't need me anymore. I promise. There are no other copies of the formula. I swear it."

Aguado raised an eyebrow, then motioned for Alvarez to follow him out of the room. The two men walked slowly through the rickety front door and out into the trampled patch of weeds that carpeted the small courtyard in front of the lab.

"What the hell is he talking about?" Aguado half-whispered.

Alvarez shrugged. "No idea, but I don't like the sound of it."

"Does he think there's a copy of the formula in the envelope?"

"Maybe it's there and we can't see it," Alvarez said. "These scientists are smart. Maybe he encoded it or something."

Aguado looked back, skeptical. "Maybe. But I don't think so. In fact, I don't think he knows what's in that envelope."

Alvarez shrugged. "Maybe, but either way, he's made a copy of the formula. We need to find out where it is."

"Agreed," Aguado said. "Let's keep him talking and see how this plays out."

Their sidebar complete, Aguado and Alvarez returned to

the lab. Martin had stemmed the flow of tears and now sat quietly in the center of the room, head hung low.

Aguado shook the envelope in front of his face. "I want you to tell me every single detail about the contents of this envelope."

"And be honest, Felix," Alvarez chimed in. "Because there are other ways we can get the details from you."

A frozen shiver went through Martin's body, and he forced himself to take a deep breath. "I promise, all I wanted was an insurance policy. So, I put a copy of the formula for Azúcar on the drive and wrote a letter explaining what it was."

Aguado's jaw tightened, and he felt the urge to slap the cowering fool seated in front of him. "And who were you going to give this insurance policy to?"

Martin was instantly glad he'd waited to address the envelope. If Aguado knew it was meant for the DEA, he'd probably be dead already. "I was just going to rent a locker at one of those mailbox stores and keep it there. I promise I wasn't going to use it."

"And where is the drive now?" Aguado pressed.

A look of confusion crossed Martin's face. "It's in the envelope."

Aguado had heard enough. "The only thing in this envelope is a goddamn baseball contract for someone named Daniel Rincon!" He removed the papers from the packet and slammed them on the counter next to Martin.

Martin eyed the documents in disbelief. "I've...I've never seen those before, Jefe."

"So where is the *real* envelope, Felix?" A vein pulsed in Aguado's forehead.

"I—I don't know," Martin stammered.

He heard a click and turned, now staring straight down the barrel of a nine-millimeter pistol. "Where is it,

Felix?" Alvarez snarled, pressing the gun into Martin's forehead.

The realization hit Martin like the delivery van he'd narrowly avoided in front of the cafe.

*The other envelope*, he thought.

He must have grabbed the wrong envelope after crashing into the group at the restaurant. Now he'd spilled his guts for nothing—Aguado had never even known about the drive. A wave of nausea swept through his stomach, and he turned his head and vomited on the floor.

Aguado and Alvarez watched in disgust.

Spit still dripping from his lips, Martin looked up at the men. With an uncontrollable tremble in his voice, he said, "When the guards were chasing me, I crashed into some people eating dinner at a cafe. I got up and saw there were two envelopes, but I only had time to grab one of them." He lowered his gaze back to the puddle of puke on the floor. "The envelopes must have gotten switched."

The tears returned—this time accompanied by giant heaving sobs.

"Keep him here until we find that drive," Aguado instructed Alvarez. "And make sure he doesn't have an escape plan this time."

---

"What does it say?" Anna asked, breaking the awkward silence at the table.

"It's a letter from someone named Felix Martin." Reynolds began reading the letter out loud:

*To Whom it May Concern,*
*My name is Felix Martin. I'm an Amer-*

ican chemist who has been abducted by the Sinaloa Cartel. They have forced me to develop a formula for a new street drug called Azúcar, one that can't be detected by U.S. Customs Agents. I've included a copy of the formula on the enclosed thumb drive. Please have one of your analysts verify its authenticity.

Now that the formula is complete, I fear that my life is in danger. If you're reading this, I am most likely dead already. The man responsible for my death is Arturo Aguado. He is the head of the Sinaloa Cartel and oversees the day-to-day operations of the organization.

Aguado's second in command is a man named Miguel Alvarez. Alvarez directs the muscle behind the Cartel and carries out Aguado's orders. These men are responsible for a huge percentage of the illegal drug traffic coming into the United States.

If Azúcar is allowed to cross the border, it will cause a plague of addiction like the United States has never seen. I am not proud of my actions, but I hope this information will aid in the capture of Aguado and Alvarez, as well as stop Azúcar from ever being manufactured and distributed.

Sincerely,

*Felix Martin*

Reynolds flipped over the paper. It was blank on the back side.

"This is bad," he said, a somber expression replacing the smile he'd worn just moments ago. "The guy on the bike must've grabbed the wrong envelope." Reynolds ran a hand through his hair. *Of all the bad luck.*

"The cartel is very dangerous, Dillon," Anna said, lowering her voice to a whisper. "What if they find out we have this information?"

As if suddenly remembering Danny was sitting next to them, both Anna and Reynolds looked at the boy. His face was a mixture of disappointment and fear.

"It's going to be okay, Mijo," Anna assured him.

"Yeah, Danny. We're going to figure this out," Reynolds interjected. "I think we ought to head back to the Academy though. It's going to be dark soon."

He eyed Anna, who nodded in agreement as the trio rose from the table and headed toward the Corolla.

If the drive to the restaurant had felt long, the drive back felt like an eternity. Not a word was spoken as they made their way back to the Academy, each mulling over the problem that had literally landed in their lap.

Finally, the car slowed to a stop at the gate of the Academy and was granted entrance by the guard. Anna eased the vehicle in front of the main doors and placed the gearshift in park.

As he and Danny exited the vehicle, Reynolds said, "Danny, I'll meet you inside. I need to talk to your mom for a minute."

"Okay." The boy shuffled slowly into the building.

Reynolds leaned into the passenger window. "Anna, I

didn't want to say anything in front of Danny, but those contracts have his name all over them. If the cartel gets ahold of our envelope, it's only a matter of time before someone comes looking for him."

He paused, carefully piecing together his next words. "I can only assume Felix Martin was the guy on the bike. If the men from the truck caught him ..." His voice trailed off.

Anna slowly nodded in agreement, her coffee brown eyes returning Reynold's solemn gaze. She knew what the cartel did to people in situations like this and it never ended well.

"What do you propose we do?" she asked.

Reynolds exhaled. "I was afraid you were going to ask me that."

---

Sitting in his office at the produce warehouse, Alvarez took a sip of Patron from a small glass on his desk. The liquor sent a warm sensation through his chest and into his gut.

After the interrogation of Felix Martin, finding this Daniel Rincon had become priority number one for Alvarez and the rest of the Cartel. Chances were, Rincon didn't even have the drive—the envelope probably got lost or thrown away at the restaurant.

But Alvarez knew this was too important to leave to chance. He had to find this Rincon, and fast. But first he needed some help from an old friend.

Alvarez grabbed the phone sitting on his desk and flipped through his contacts. He scrolled until he found the name he was looking for—Rafael Zapata—a legendary cartel heavyweight.

Alvarez thought back to the first time he'd worked with Zapata. They were both much younger men at the time. Jefe had paired them up to snuff out a small rival cartel that was gaining strength in Sinaloa.

The rivals operated out of an abandoned airport on the outskirts of Culiacán, the capital city of Sinaloa. The fledgling operation was housed in an old airplane hangar, where they cooked meth day and night.

The building was made of rust-pocked corrugated steel, and featured a massive set of double doors that hung from tracks on the front of the structure. Two guards stood in front of the doors, one fat, one skinny, each with an AR-15 slung across his shoulder.

Seeing the single entrance and the barred windows gave Alvarez an idea.

He and Zapata retuned the next night with a plan. Alvarez crept silently to the side of the building, a long duffel bag over his left shoulder. Meanwhile, Zapata took a swig from a half empty bottle of tequila, then doused the front of his shirt with the rest of the liquor.

He began stumbling towards the guards, singing the words to *Mexico Lindo*, an old mariachi tune. In his finest drunken impression, he bellowed, "México lindo y querido, si muero lejos de ti que digan que estoy dormido. (*Mexico, beautiful and dear, if I die far from you, let them say that I am asleep*").

The guards rose and stared at Zapata as he stumbled toward them, belching, then launching into the next verse.

"What are you doing?" the skinny guard called to him.

"Singing," Zapata replied bluntly, and took another swig from the bottle.

The guard looked at Zapata in disgust. "I can smell your stench from here, cabron. Beat it before I put a bullet in your worthless head."

The distraction was just enough to allow Alvarez to slip behind both guards. The muffled *tink* of a suppressed nine-millimeter Sig Sauer echoed off the warehouse doors, and the fat guard dropped.

The skinny guard turned to see his fallen comrade, then whirled back to Zapata, eyes wide. But now, instead of a tequila bottle, Zapata was holding an identical suppressed Sig Sauer. He fired the weapon and the skinny guard dropped to his knees, then collapsed in a lifeless heap.

Quickly, Alvarez retrieved the duffel bag from the side of the building. Inside was a thick steel chain and a rectangular black plastic case. Each man retrieved an item: Alvarez the chain, Zapata the case.

Alvarez began looping the chain through the handles on the double doors, ensuring they couldn't be opened from the inside.

Zapata opened the plastic case and removed the FN Herstal grenade launcher from inside. He expertly extended the stock and slid open a large tube at the front of the weapon, then inserted a forty-millimeter shell.

Both men walked to the first of the small bar covered windows on the side of the building.

They'd scouted the hangar yesterday and knew the lab took up most of the space inside the building. A series of PVC curtains were crudely hung between makeshift two by four posts, forming a plastic perimeter around the lab. Outside the curtain, a round table with two metal folding chairs stood towards the rear of the building, where a pair of men sat and played cards. The rest of the space was filled with various drums, buckets, and boxes of ingredients used to manufacture meth.

Alvarez glanced quickly through the window. He could see shadows moving behind the translucent curtains of the lab. Tonight, the same two men were again seated at the table playing cards.

He held up three fingers, then two, then one.

Zapata rose and braced the grenade launcher against his right shoulder. Positioning the barrel through the bars, he fired a single shot through the dust covered glass and into the center of the building. A perfect shot.

The explosion rocked the thin steel walls of the hangar. The plastic curtains caught fire instantly and bodies began frantically clawing through the flames. A second explosion swept through the building as a tank of chemicals ignited, sending a firestorm at the card-playing men.

It was utter chaos. The men inside the building pried at the double doors—to no avail. Others grabbed at the bars that covered the windows, searing their flesh on the red-hot steel.

"Let's get out of here," Alvarez called to Zapata.

But Zapata didn't move. He simply stood there in a murderous trance, staring through the window. He watched intently as men reached through the bars, screaming in agony as they burned alive.

"Zapata!" Alvarez called again. "Let's go!"

Zapata awoke from the trance and stretched his neck from side to side, as if working out a bothersome kink. Calmly, he placed the grenade launcher back in the case and began whistling the melody of *Mexico Lindo*, then looked at Alvarez with a satisfied smile. "You want to grab something to eat?"

---

Alvarez and Zapata stood quietly in front of the Bohemia Birrieria, examining the building. The restaurant was a popular tourist destination because of its proximity to the Malecon—a thirteen-mile seawall that ran along the main bay of Mazatlán.

But at nine o'clock in the morning, there was only a

smattering of customers here and there, mostly stopping in for a Bloody Mary or a Mimosa before heading to the beach.

The building was well-maintained, looking newer than most in the area. Its creamsicle-colored walls were lined with archways trimmed in robin's egg blue. An intricately scrolled wrought-iron railing ran along the second-story balcony that overlooked a small patio below.

Zapata scanned the patio. It was dotted with circular tables covered in tangerine-colored tablecloths and set with matching orange napkins. There were palm trees spaced every few feet and large fans had been mounted to their trunks to keep the patrons cool in the tropical heat.

As he looked up at the fans, Zapata spotted a wrought-iron arm extending from above one of the archways on the first floor. The arm held a gas lantern, its blue pilot flame barely visible in the bright sun. Attached to the lower portion of the arm was a small camera with a black plastic dome beneath it. There was a flashing green LED dot on the side of the camera, indicating, presumably, that it was recording.

Zapata nudged Alvarez and looked up. "We need to see that camera footage."

Alvarez agreed, and the men started into the restaurant, weaving through the tables into the air-conditioned indoor dining space.

A petite young girl, not more than eighteen years old, greeted them with a smile. "Hola," she said. "How many today?"

"We need to see the manager," Alvarez grunted.

A look of concern immediately replaced her smile. "Let me see if I can find him. Please wait here."

The girl returned moments later with a heavy-set man in a dark suit and red tie. The buttons on his suit coat were straining against his distended belly, and his tie looked as if it was slowly strangling him.

"Can I help you, gentlemen?"

"I need to see your camera footage from last night," Alvarez stated.

"Is there a problem?" the manager replied.

"No problem. We just need to see the footage from last night."

The manager stuck a finger in the collar of his shirt, trying to give his thick neck some breathing room. "Gentlemen, do you have some identification? Are you police officers?"

Alvarez lifted the bottom of his western shirt, revealing the nine-millimeter Sig Sauer in the waistband of his jeans.

The man looked at the pistol and gasped.

Zapata's hand shot up and grabbed the manager's fatty neck, squeezing into the folds in search of the man's windpipe. The man began to choke and gasp.

"Take us to the cameras, fat man."

The manager nodded vehemently, and Zapata released his grip.

Wheezing, the manager turned and headed toward the back of the restaurant, gesturing for Alvarez and Zapata to follow him. He stopped at a locked door just opposite the entrance to the kitchen. He removed a set of keys from his pocket, fumbling for the right one before inserting it into the lock.

The room was a closet more than it was an office. There were no windows, and the space was dimly lit by a single lightbulb. A cheap desk lined the left wall, flanked by an office copier and a tan filing cabinet. The walls were covered in calendars, food safety bulletins and a myriad of other mind-numbing documents.

Atop the filing cabinet sat a small television monitor,

which was separated into four squares, each showing a different camera view of the restaurant.

"Last night around five," Alvarez snapped. "The camera on the patio. Start there."

The manager seated himself at the desk and pecked at the keyboard, pulling up the program for the cameras. He navigated to another screen and selected the day and time Alvarez had requested.

The four squares disappeared, and the monitor switched to a full screen view of the patio. The time stamp on the recording read 5:00.

"Speed it up," Alvarez snapped again.

The manager punched another key, and the video accelerated.

The men watched in silence as diners came and went, waiters took orders and bus boys cleared tables.

Alvarez remembered Martin had said there were three people seated at the table he'd collided with. But the video showed only couples on the patio, with one large group in the corner—no trios.

A few more seconds passed, and a new group walked into the picture. A gringo, a Mexican woman, and a teenaged kid.

They seated themselves and began talking. Within seconds, a body hurtled into the frame from the edge of the monitor, crashing into the table and landing on the cement patio.

"Pause it," Alvarez demanded.

The video stopped, and Alvarez and Zapata exchanged glances. This was their group.

"Run it at normal speed."

The picture continued as Martin collected himself and grabbed an envelope, then took off down the street, followed by the cartel guards.

The manager looked back as if to say, *Seen enough?* But Alvarez grunted. "Keep going."

They watched as bus boys cleared the wreckage and reset the table. The manager appeared in the frame shortly after, gesturing apologetically with his hands then retreating into the restaurant.

As the diners seated themselves back at the table, Alvarez stared intently at the monitor. The gringo picked up the envelope and opened it, then dumped something out onto the table.

*The drive,* he thought.

The man looked like he was reading the letter—and his lips were moving. He was reading the letter aloud.

"Shit," Alvarez muttered to himself.

They had to find these idiots before they told someone else—everyone else. But that wouldn't be the end of their problems. It would be easy to deal with the woman and the kid. But the white guy? That would be a different story. Two Mexicans go missing in Sinaloa and it's just another day. An American goes missing and people start asking questions.

Alvarez continued watching the video as the gringo put the drive and the letter back in the envelope and the trio rose to leave. They zigzagged through the tables and out to the street, stopping at a tan colored Toyota Corolla.

"Pause it," Alvarez ordered.

He squinted as if to clarify the grainy footage, barely making out the rear license plate—VHA-79-20. Alvarez punched the numbers and letters into his phone and clicked save.

"We're done here," Alvarez said to Zapata.

The men left the restaurant to report their findings to Aguado.

# CHAPTER 10

Aguado sat quietly in his lavish study, sipping a tiny cup of rich black espresso. He was so close to realizing his dream. With the formula for Azúcar complete, manufacture and distribution were the only boxes left to check.

Once they were up and running, the cash would flow in by the billions. Not a single shipment would be lost to the U.S. Customs and Border Patrol. No more elaborate schemes to hide product among other shipments. He would operate with the freedom of any other legitimate businessman. His trucks would cross the border filled with product, return home safely, and repeat the process.

But he had to tie up this loose end. "Daniel Rincon," Aguado muttered, looking at the paperwork lying on his desk. If that imbecile Martin had indeed switched the envelopes last night, then this Daniel Rincon must have taken the other one.

The phone on his desk buzzed, and Aguado put it to his ear.

"Sí."

"Jefe, we're headed your way now. We've got some information on Rincon."

"Good, get here as soon as you can."

The line went dead. Ten minutes later Alvarez and Zapata walked into the study and seated themselves in the chairs before the gilt wood desk.

"What did you find out?" Aguado asked.

"Daniel Rincon is a kid, maybe fifteen or sixteen years old. And he was with a woman and a younger white guy."

Aguado gestured for Alvarez to continue.

"The white guy opened the envelope."

"Shit." Aguado knew it was unlikely, but he'd hoped to retrieve the envelope unscathed and unopened. "Did he read the letter?"

"Worse," Alvarez replied slowly.

Aguado sank back in his chair with a grunt. "How much worse?"

"We're not a hundred percent sure, but we think the gringo read the letter out loud. If he did, the woman and the kid heard it for sure."

"And anyone else within earshot," Aguado added. He slammed his fist on the desk causing the nearly empty cup of espresso to overturn and spatter dark droplets across the papers that littered its surface. "That's going to complicate things."

Alvarez and Zapata knew better than to speak when Aguado was agitated. They simply sat quietly and waited for instructions.

A long silence passed while Aguado calmed himself, breathing in deeply through his nose and exhaling through his mouth.

"Our number one priority is getting that drive back," he said.

"We got a plate number from the car the woman was

driving," Alvarez replied. "I can have one of our police officer friends in town get us a name to go with it."

Aguado looked up and nodded. "Good. Start there. I want to be updated every step of the way on this. And if you find the woman, bring her here immediately."

"Yes, Jefe," Alvarez replied.

---

Reynolds stood hunched over the passenger side window of Anna's Corolla. "I think we should take the envelope to the police."

Anna shook her head. "No. The police here are just as corrupt as the Cartel."

She knew the depth of police corruption in Sinaloa firsthand. Years ago, when Danny was a baby, she and Danny's father, Juan, had gotten into an argument. He'd come home from the bar drunk one night and began pushing and shoving Anna, complaining there was nothing to eat.

When she told him to leave, Juan screamed and told her she couldn't kick him out of his own home. The shoves turned to slaps, and eventually to punches.

In a desperate attempt to end the beating, Anna lay on the floor motionless, pretending to be knocked unconscious. Eventually it worked. The blows stopped, and she listened through the ache in her head as Juan shuffled into the bedroom to pass out in a drunken stupor.

Bloodied and bruised, she'd fought through the pain and gathered herself enough to call the police.

They arrived, albeit four hours later, and Anna explained the events that had taken place that night. Juan, still half-drunk and hearing the commotion from the bedroom, emerged and immediately began pleading his innocence.

A young officer had taken Anna to the kitchen while Juan and an older officer talked in the living room. As the younger officer questioned Anna, she watched over his shoulder as Juan slipped the older officer a handful of pesos. The man smiled and shook Juan's hand, then yelled for the younger officer to leave, telling him there was nothing further they could do.

She couldn't believe what she'd just witnessed. Her husband had nearly beaten her to death and now he'd simply paid the police to leave. No handcuffs, no arrest, and certainly no protection.

Of course, another beating ensued shortly thereafter. And after that night, Anna vowed two things: one, she would do whatever it took to leave Juan and escape with her son. And two, she would never trust the police again.

Reynolds could see the fear and pain in Anna's eyes when she spoke about the police. That look was all he needed to scrap the idea.

"Okay, so we can't go to the cops," Reynolds said. "Who else do you trust in this town?"

"No one," she replied. "Sinaloa is a very corrupt place. The police, the politicians—they're all dishonest. Most of them would sell us out for a few pesos."

Reynolds exhaled, frustrated with the lack of options. This wasn't a world he was familiar with. Back home, law and order were things he took for granted. Here, they were fanciful ideals, foolishly clung to by the weak and naïve.

"Listen, I'm sure we're blowing this out of proportion," Reynolds lied. "Let me talk to Ed tomorrow and see what he thinks we should do."

Anna looked skeptical. "Do you trust him?"

"He's the uncle of one of my buddies back in the states. And he's always been straight with me. Besides, I'm running out of ideas as the moment."

Anna couldn't help but agree. They weren't exactly flush with options right now.

Reynolds continued, "Ed's probably gone home for the night, and I don't want to discuss this over the phone. I'll have to talk to him first thing in the morning. In the meantime, though, I don't think it's a good idea for you to go home." Reynolds held out his hands. "Just as a precaution."

"I agree. I have a friend from work that lives nearby. I can stay with her tonight."

"Okay, good," Reynolds quickly replied. "Let's meet back here in the morning around nine o'clock. I'll have talked to Ed by then and we can figure a way out of this."

"I'll see you in the morning then," Anna replied, then pulled away from the curb and eased the car through the exit.

Reynolds watched her leave, then turned and headed into the building. Maybe he'd get lucky and catch Ed here late on a Friday night. Probably not, but it was worth the short walk to his office.

The executive floor was dark, the lights turned off by the building's automatic timers. Reynolds flipped a switch on the wall and a row of fluorescent bulbs buzzed to life, illuminating a path to Ed's corner office at the back of the room. Reynolds peeked his head through the office door, where he saw a small lamp had been left on, casting a dim light over the desk and revealing the empty chair behind it.

*Damn, have to catch him in the morning,* Reynolds thought, and walked to the desk to shut off the lamp.

As he reached for the switch, Reynolds glanced at a stack of paperwork on the desk. The first sheet read LOAN AGREEMENT in bold letters across the top of the paper. He continued reading: it was an agreement between a company called Eldorado Finance and the parents of Alejandro Avila. The terms specified the company would loan the Avilas the sum of one hundred thousand dollars, to be repaid at an interest rate of eight percent—per month.

Reynolds' eyes nearly bulged out of his head as he read the verbiage again. *Eight Percent per month?*

The most unethical loans in the states were in the twenty-five to thirty percent range per *year*, and people could rarely dig out of those holes. But eight percent a month? That was racketeering.

As he thumbed through the stack, Reynolds counted four more contracts between Eldorado Finance and other players' families. The amounts, varied but the interest rate was always the same: eight percent each month.

He wondered what Ed had to do with all this. Why did he have this paperwork on his desk? And why in the hell were these people agreeing to such ridiculous terms?

And then it flashed through his head, the conversation he'd overheard earlier in the day when Ed was on the phone. "Yes, I know the interest is high, but you'll easily be able to pay it all back when Alejandro gets his signing bonus."

The reality struck him like a wrecking ball. Ed must be a part of this Eldorado Finance company. He was issuing the loans against the players' signing bonuses, and the parents were spending the money before it ever got paid.

But why? Ed had never mentioned the loans before. He'd told Reynolds the Academy got paid by developing players and acting as their agent when the player got signed. And of course, the less talented players paid to train there, but this loan scheme was never discussed.

To make matters worse, what Reynolds knew and what the parents didn't was that, many times, the bonuses wouldn't get paid out at all. If the player was younger than sixteen years old, the teams couldn't officially sign a contract with him, so they made "off-the-record agreements" instead.

These agreements made the player and his family feel like they were under contract, even though they weren't.

Of course, the agreements were completely unenforceable. It was a low risk, high upside proposition for Major League teams. If the player didn't pan out by the time he was sixteen, they would reduce the signing bonus or even pull the offer completely, leaving the family in a mountain of debt.

Reynolds knew Alejandro Avila was only fourteen. His parents would have to pay eight percent per month on the hundred-thousand-dollar loan for nearly two years. He was no math major, but the amount of interest was astronomical.

The whole notion gave Reynolds pause. It just didn't seem like something Ed would do. Maybe talking to Ed about the envelope wasn't the right thing to do after all. If he was running this loan scheme, what else could he be hiding?

Out of options, Reynolds shook the thought from his mind. He knew Ed to be a good guy, there had to be an explanation for all of this. But that would have to come some other time. The priority now was to ensure Danny and Anna's safety.

Reynolds clicked off the desk lamp, reassuring himself that talking to Ed in the morning was the right thing to do.

---

Alvarez repeated the digits into the phone, V-H-A-7-9-2-0. There was silence on the other end, save for a flurry of staccato strokes on a keyboard.

"It's registered to an Anna Rincon of Villa Unión."

"You got an address?" Alvarez asked.

"Sí, it's listed as Margarita Maza de Juárez 202."

Alvarez clicked off the phone and looked at Zapata. "She lives in Villa Unión. It's about thirty minutes from here."

The men exited the small office at the back of the produce warehouse and walked toward a gleaming black Cadillac Escalade parked near one of the loading docks.

It was early afternoon when they arrived at the Rincon residence, and people milled about in the streets. Storekeepers swept the entries in front of their shops while groups of women toted bags of groceries down the sidewalk.

Alvarez pulled the Escalade to a stop in front of the apartment. A man across the street stood on a plastic five-gallon bucket and wrenched on the engine of an old Chevy pickup. He looked up, gawking at the shiny SUV, then locked eyes with Alvarez and quickly returned his attention back to the tired engine.

Alvarez pushed through the narrow metal gate, then through a red wooden door that opened into a small courtyard in the center of the apartment building.

"Two Zero Two," he said to Zapata, and the men began ascending the corroded metal staircase. Their heavy boot steps echoed against the walls of the courtyard below.

Alvarez tried the door—locked, as expected. He turned to Zapata and nodded. Without a word, the man sent a violent front kick into the door, splintering the wooden casing and ripping the lock from its seat.

An old woman in a white apron poked her head out from the apartment next door and quickly retreated inside at the sight of Alvarez and Zapata, guns drawn.

One by one they entered the apartment and scanned the room, weapons out and following their gaze. The apartment was quiet as the men crept from room to room, clearing each before holstering their weapons.

"Start back there," Alvarez said to Zapata.

Zapata headed to the back of the apartment and

through one of the bedroom doors while Alvarez began searching the living room. He pulled a large tactical knife from his boot and began slicing the already tattered couch. Synthetic stuffing burst from the cushions and fell into piles on the floor.

He continued his search in the kitchen, opening the flimsy cupboard doors and removing boxes and bottles—dumping the contents on the cracked linoleum. Moving to the small humming refrigerator, he opened it to reveal a glass pitcher of milk and a cardboard container of orange juice. He poured both on the floor—the liquids mixing with the ingredients from the cupboards to form a slushy stew on the floor.

Zapata continued searching the bedrooms, slicing through tired mattresses and pillows and rummaging through the cheap particle board dressers, emptying the drawers one by one. Finally, he moved to the bathroom, searching the small cabinet beneath the sink, then the shelves above it.

After thirty minutes of ransacking the apartment, they had found nothing. No drive, no envelope—nothing.

"It's like searching for a needle in a haystack," Alvarez said to Zapata, and replaced the knife in his boot. "That drive could be anywhere."

"What now?" Zapata asked.

"I'll call Jefe, see what he thinks."

Alvarez punched Aguado's name on the contact list and put the phone to his ear.

"Sí."

"Jefe, she's not here. We searched the place and didn't find the drive or the envelope either."

"No matter," Aguado replied sharply. "Get back here as soon as you can. I've got something."

Aguado had read through the paperwork in the envelope briefly last night, but he'd been tired and needed a good night's sleep. Maybe a second pass could help steer him toward his target.

Now he scanned one of documents more closely. It was an offer letter from the Minnesota Twins. He'd seen countless contracts before, and this one was formatted similarly, chocked with fancy words and numbered paragraphs that spelled out the terms of the agreement in mind-numbing detail.

In exchange for a signing bonus in the amount of one million dollars, the Minnesota Twins would own the rights to this Daniel Rincon throughout his minor league career and the first three years of his tenure in the Major Leagues.

The contract contained countless paragraphs of legal mumbo jumbo which Aguado quickly skimmed over. But as he continued reading, his eyes stopped on the last page—a document titled *Addendum A*.

*The Player hereby employs the Academia de Béisbol de Sinaloa and the Academia de Béisbol de Sinaloa hereby agrees to act as management (and agent through Ed Hernandez Sports Management) for the Player.*

Aguado looked up from the document. How could he have missed this last night?

"The Academia de Béisbol de Sinaloa," he said under his breath. He vaguely remembered dealing with someone at the Academy in the past.

As he scanned his memory, the phone on his desk buzzed.

"Sí."

Aguado listened for a short while then said sharply, "No

matter. Get back here as soon as you can. I've got something."

Shortly after, Alvarez and Zapata were seated before him, awaiting instructions.

Aguado put a hand on the document he'd been reading and slid it across the desk to Alvarez. "Miguel, don't we know someone at the Academia de Béisbol de Sinaloa?"

Alvarez pondered the question for a moment. "Let me check."

He punched up a directory of contacts on his cell phone and scrolled through the list. "Yeah, I remember this guy. We helped him out years ago when his business was in trouble. Now we run a loan racket through the place."

"What's his name?" Aguado asked.

"Ed Hernandez."

# CHAPTER 11

Bright morning sunlight streamed through the large windows of Ed Hernandez's corner office. He'd gotten an early start this Saturday to go over the loan documents one last time, before he delivered them to the lawyers.

He hated these loans. They were evil. Hernandez knew half of them would never be repaid, because the bonuses only came through half the time. If the family couldn't pay, the cartel would own them, turning the fathers into drug mules and the mothers into worse.

But he had no choice. It was his penance for taking cartel money all those years ago when the Academy was in trouble. Now, the Sinaloa Cartel expected the loans to come through every year like clockwork—no exceptions.

As he thumbed through the paperwork, there was a knock on the door. He glanced up.

"Dillon," he said, "Good morning." He returned his gaze to the loan agreements sitting on his desk.

"Morning, Ed," Reynolds replied. "Do you have a minute? I've got a situation, and I'd like to get your opinion."

Hernandez looked up with a tired half-smile. "I was just

leaving to deliver these documents. But it should only take an hour or so. Can we talk when I get back?"

Disappointed, but knowing he didn't have much of a choice, Reynolds replied, "Sure. Shoot me a text when you're back in the building."

"Will do." Hernandez said and scooped a black and silver key fob off the glass desktop.

As Reynolds sat downstairs in the cafeteria, poking at a rubbery ham and cheese omelet with his fork, he mulled the previous twenty-four hours. What a whirlwind. First the news that Danny had gotten three offers, then the dinner, the envelope, and finally the predatory loans Ed was clearly involved in.

He took a sip of coffee and immediately spit it back in the cup. Ice cold. How long had he been sitting here lost in thought?

As he rose from the plastic cafeteria chair, the phone in his pocket buzzed. It was Anna.

"Good morning," he said, trying to sound chipper.

Her voice was frantic. "Dillon, is Danny, okay?"

"Yeah, I just saw him a few minutes ago on my way to the cafeteria. Why?"

"My apartment," she said, through tears. "They broke in and destroyed everything!"

"Whoa! Hold on. Who broke into your apartment?" Reynolds replied, dazed by the news.

"I, I don't know. But they were looking for something. They tore up the couch, the mattresses. Dumped all the food on the floor. I think it's the cartel!"

*Shit. The envelope. They were looking for it.*

"I thought you were staying with a friend last night," he said. "What happened?"

Anna sniffled. "I needed some fresh clothes, so I drove

home this morning and when I walked in ..." Her voice trailed off.

"Get out of there now. Come to the Academy. You'll be safe here until we can figure something out."

Her voice whimpered into the phone. "Okay, I'll be there in thirty minutes."

*Shit, shit, shit.* If there was ever a doubt they were in trouble, that doubt had just gone out the window.

Still holding his phone, Reynolds looked down as it vibrated in his palm.

> Just got back to the Academy. I'll be in my office for the next couple of hours if you still want to talk.

Perfect timing. Ed was back. Hopefully, he would have an idea what to do.

Reynolds hustled upstairs and lowered himself into a chair facing Ed's desk, nervous energy coursing through his body. The phone call from Anna had shaken him, and his thoughts now swam with vile gangsters and corrupt cops.

"You look like shit," Hernandez said bluntly, examining Reynolds' suddenly pale face.

"Didn't get much sleep last night."

Hernandez looked surprised. "Did everything go okay with Danny yesterday?"

Reynolds shook his head. "No, it didn't."

Hernandez waited for him to continue speaking.

"Do you mind if I close the door?" Reynolds asked.

"Go ahead," Hernandez replied, his curiosity thoroughly piqued.

Reynolds rose from the chair and softly closed the heavy wooden door, not wanting to draw any unnecessary attention.

"You're making me nervous," Hernandez said as Reynolds returned to his seat.

"I'm the one that's nervous, Ed." He exhaled deeply. "I need your advice about something."

"Sure. What is it?"

As Reynolds steeled himself to describe the scene at the restaurant last night, and now the break in at Anna's apartment, a rapid knocking came from the closed office door.

Hernandez rose slowly and started toward the door. "Sorry Dillon. This must be important."

One of the younger coaches, a kid named Manuel Bacasegua, stood in the doorway—a panicked look on his face. "Ed, we've got a problem downstairs. One of the boy's fathers is pissed about something and wants to talk to you personally. He won't talk to anyone else and he's making a huge scene in the lobby."

Hernandez closed his eyes and pinched the bridge of his nose. "Okay, I'll be right down." In Ed's experience, every parent—fathers especially—knew for a fact their boy was going to go pro, probably become an All-Star or hell, most likely go to Cooperstown.

Except the notion couldn't be any farther from the truth. This was one of the premier facilities in Latin America, and only a tiny fraction of the boys that had come through here ever saw a single inning in the Major Leagues—but parents were never good at dealing with reality. Hernandez could only guess what the father downstairs was so upset about.

He looked at Dillon as he started through the doorway. "I'm sorry, Dillon. Can we pick this up in a few minutes?"

Reynolds wanted to scream. He needed to talk now. Instead, he simply muttered, "Sure, text me when you're done downstairs."

As Hernandez strode down the hallway to deal with the agitated parent, Reynolds heard a buzzing underneath a sheet of paper on the desk. As he moved the paper, he saw Hernandez had forgotten his phone. Then he saw the name pop up on the screen: Miguel Alvarez.

Wasn't that the name of the guy in Felix Martin's letter? The second in command to the boss? Reynolds couldn't remember the name of the boss, but he remembered the name Alvarez. He'd played with a guy named Alvarez in Reno, a mediocre pitcher but a heck of a bowler. The two had spent many nights together at a local bowling alley.

This couldn't be right. First the predatory loans, now Hernandez was mixed up with the cartel. What the hell was going on? Had the cartel found out where Danny was already? A thousand thoughts swirled through Reynolds' mind.

One thing was for certain now, though. Ed most certainly could not be trusted. Reynolds was suddenly glad their conversation had been interrupted. But now what was he going to do? Hernandez had been his only lifeline out of this situation. Now that lifeline had been yanked out of the water, and the sharks were circling.

He had to get Danny out of here fast, while Ed was occupied.

Reynolds hurried to his dorm room, tempering his pace to avoid attention. Once there, he snatched the manilla envelope off the narrow desk and slid it into a backpack on the floor. Next, he hurriedly wadded up a few sets of socks and underwear, a couple of t-shirts and a pair of jeans and stuffed them in the backpack.

He slung the pack over his shoulder and headed downstairs to the training facility. Reynolds had seen Danny in the batting cages earlier and hoped he'd still be there.

Winding through the facility, Reynolds avoided any and all eye contact with the other employees. His mind raced with paranoia. Was everyone here working for the cartel?

Was the whole place a front? Scenario after scenario ran through his head, each one more outlandish than the last.

Finally, Reynolds made his way to the batting cages and spotted Danny, as predicted, taking batting practice from one of the pitching machines.

"Danny!" he yelled.

The boy turned, startled, and looked back at Reynolds. "Yeah?"

"We need to go. Your mom is going to be here any minute."

Danny looked puzzled, but saw the look of concern on Reynolds' face and didn't ask questions.

Before he could begin loading up his bat bag, Reynolds barked, "Leave it. We'll get it later."

Danny knew something was wrong. He'd grown up in the streets of a rough town. You learn things about life on the streets. Things they don't teach in school—a sixth sense for trouble. And now Danny was worried. He'd never seen Reynolds act this way.

As instructed, he left the bat bag and his other gear lying on the turf and followed Reynolds to the lobby.

Luckily, Ed was still occupied with the angry father. The two men had retreated to a small seating area in the lobby's corner and Reynolds watched as the father's hands gestured wildly.

Reynolds and Danny exited the building unseen and began walking toward the perimeter. To the side of the guard shack, a narrow gate opened into the street. Reynolds pushed through it and motioned for Danny to follow. As they headed down the sidewalk, he dialed Anna's number again.

"Hola," she said.

"We're out-front of the Academy heading west. There's an Oxxo right across the street, we'll be inside."

As they continued walking, Reynolds felt a tug on his arm. "Dillon, what's going on?" Danny asked, uncertainty in his voice.

"I'll explain when your mom gets here. She should be close."

Reynolds milled about in the convenience store, browsing the candy isle while searching his phone intently. Pressing a button, he put the phone to his ear.

Danny walked to the refrigerators at the back of the store. The shelves were lined with ice-cold bottles of water, soda, and beer. He glanced up at the convex surveillance mirror in the corner and could see Reynolds talking on the phone. He was speaking rapidly and didn't look pleased with the voice on the other end.

Reynolds hung up the phone and put it back in his pocket, checking out the window for the umpteenth time since they'd entered the store. Finally, he saw the rusty Corolla pull into the parking lot and stop at a gas pump.

"Let's go!" Reynolds called to Danny.

The pair approached the car, Reynolds taking the front seat this time and Danny the rear.

"What's going on, Dillon?" Anna asked, a fearful expression on her face.

"Just drive, I'll fill you in along the way."

"Where are we headed?"

"The U.S. Consulate," he said. "In Guadalajara."

---

"Where have you been?" The voice on the other end of the phone was agitated and impatient. "I've called you three times."

"I'm sorry, Miguel," Hernandez explained. "I was dealing

with an issue downstairs and didn't have my phone with me."

"We've got a problem with one of your players."

The statement caught him off guard, and a sent electric current of panic through Hernandez's body. "Who?"

"Daniel Rincon."

"Danny?" Ed said, his voice now a mixture of surprise and confusion. "What's the problem?"

Alvarez explained the events of the previous night, the interaction with Felix Martin and the mix-up with the envelopes.

*That's what Dillon wanted to talk about.* Hernandez cupped his hand to his forehead, now slick with perspiration.

"Who were the woman and the gringo with Rincon last night?" Alvarez asked.

"The woman is his mother and the gringo's name is Dillon Reynolds. He's a coach here at the Academy."

"We need to talk to all of them immediately."

"Of course," Hernandez replied. "I saw Dillon and Danny this morning. We'll have to locate the mother though."

"Do it," Alvarez barked. "When you've got them, meet me at the warehouse. I'll be in the back."

The line went dead. Hernandez knew better than to ask what was in that envelope, though now he was curious. He also knew that, if Alvarez was this concerned, it must be important.

Hernandez hurried through the facility, first to the batting cages, then to the cafeteria and finally to both Reynolds' and Danny's dorm rooms. They were nowhere to be found.

He'd seen Danny's bat bag lying in front of the batting

cage, the familiar number *20* embroidered on the side, but the boy was gone.

Removing the phone from his pocket, Hernandez texted Reynolds:

> Need to talk to you ASAP. Where are you?

The search exhausted, Hernandez decided to check building's surveillance cameras while he waited for Reynolds to text back.

He quickly returned to his office and punched up a program on his computer. A few clicks later, the screen filled with dozens of squares of Academy surveillance footage.

The last time he'd seen Reynolds was around eight o'clock that morning, which meant he and Danny had left shortly after that. Hernandez scanned the footage from earlier that morning, finally stopping on the camera that covered the batting cages.

Running the video slowly forward, he watched as Danny took batting practice. The kid's swing was coming along nicely.

Hernandez shook his head and frowned. Here he was searching surveillance video at the behest of the world's most powerful drug cartel, yet he was still enamored with the mechanics of a good swing. Old habits die hard.

As Hernandez continued watching, Reynolds strode into the frame looking frantic and hurried. He said something to Danny, and the two walked out of the camera's view. It looked like they'd exited the training facility and were heading toward the lobby.

He clicked a box that played footage from the lobby and enlarged the screen. Sure enough, the pair entered the lobby walking quickly and slipped through the front doors, vanishing into the parking lot.

He could see himself and the agitated father talking in the video's background screen and Hernandez silently cursed the father. The man had cost him the chance to prevent an avalanche of problems.

Another click of a button, and the screen switched to a panoramic view of the building's exterior shot from a camera above the front entrance. Hernandez hit fast forward until the images of Reynolds and Danny entered the frame. He slowed the video and watched as they approached the guard shack, then exited the facility through a small gate and began walking down the boulevard that ran parallel to the Academy. The pair turned and crossed the busy street, then disappeared from view.

Hernandez pulled the phone from his pocket and dialed.

"Sí."

"We've got a problem."

## CHAPTER 12

"Guadalajara?" Anna gasped. "Why do we need to go to the Consulate? Did you talk to Ed?"

"I tried to," Reynolds said. "But just as we sat down to talk there was an issue at the Academy and Ed had to hurry downstairs to deal with it. When he left, he didn't take his phone, and I heard it buzzing under some papers, so I picked it up. When I looked at the screen, it read Miguel Alvarez."

Anna paused. The name sounded familiar, but she couldn't quite place it.

Reynolds saw the look on Anna's face and answered the question before she could ask: "It's the cartel guy from the letter. The second in command to the boss."

"Why would he be calling Ed?" Anna asked, now more confused than before.

"Last night I went up to Ed's office to see if he was still there. He wasn't, but I saw some papers on his desk. They were loan agreements between some of the players' parents and a company called Eldorado Finance—*very* high interest loans that are *very* dangerous for the families. If I had to guess, Ed's in business with the cartel to finance the loans. It's the only connection I can think of that makes sense."

Anna absorbed this. "But why can't we just go to the Consulate in Mazatlán? Guadalajara is hours from here."

"No good," Reynolds replied. "I spoke to the Mazatlán office while Danny and I were waiting in the store. The guy said we need to go to the Guadalajara Consulate, since they have a branch for the DEA there."

Reynolds paused and pulled his phone from his front pocket—there was a text from Ed.

> Need to talk to you ASAP. Where are you?

"It's Ed." He looked intently at Anna. "He knows Danny and I are gone."

Danny had remained silent in the backseat but now spoke up, his voice taking a mature tone Reynold's hadn't heard before. "Guys, what's going on?" He demanded.

Anna calmed herself, hoping Danny would do the same. "Danny, the letter in that envelope last night was evidence that could hurt the cartel."

"I know mom, I'm not dumb. But they don't even know we have it. Why don't we just ditch the envelope and pretend like we never saw anything?"

Reynolds cut in, "Because Danny, they *do* know we have it."

Danny's eyes narrowed, and Anna continued. "They broke into our apartment yesterday looking for the envelope. If they can find out where we live, it won't be long until they figure out you're a player at the Academy. And if Ed is involved somehow, we need to stay far away from that place."

Danny's heart sunk. What about the offers, his baseball career, his friends at the Academy?

And then guilt crept over him as he thought about his mother and her safety. He knew exactly what the cartel was capable of. Last year in school, one of the boys began delivering packages for a local gangster after class.

As the story went, he'd screwed up a particularly important delivery, and the gangster had beaten him so badly the boy didn't return to school for weeks. When he did return, his face still showed the yellow and purple remnants of heavy bruising around his eyes and cheeks, and his nose was tilted to one side with a large scab across the bridge.

If that's what they did to a delivery boy, Danny could only speculate what they would do to someone who had vital information that could hurt the cartel.

Reynolds clearly sensed his unease. "Look Danny, we'll go to the Consulate, and we'll get this figured out. I'm sure they'll be able to help us."

Danny didn't look convinced, but nodded anyway.

Reynolds' phone buzzed again—Ed was calling. He quickly declined the call.

Seconds later, a text popped up on the screen.

> Dillon, what's going on? Are you in some kind of trouble? I'll do anything I can to help you, just come back to the Academy.

Reynolds read the message and shook his head. *Yeah right.*

---

"What do you mean they're gone?" Alvarez spat into the phone.

"I checked the surveillance footage," said Hernandez. "Dillon and Danny slipped out of the building this morning before you called. The video just caught them crossing the Boulevard before they left the camera's view."

"Did they have the envelope?"

"I don't know. Dillon was wearing a backpack, but the kid wasn't carrying anything." Hernandez could sense Alvarez's growing impatience. "I called and texted him too. No answer."

"Do you think the gringo knows about our association with the Academy?"

"No way," Hernandez said. "I think he was trying to tell me about the envelope when I got pulled away this morning. Dillon trusts me."

"Then why did they leave? Where did they go?" Alvarez's voice was thick with venom.

"I'm not sure. I know Dillon doesn't have a car, so they'll be on foot—unless Danny's mother picked them up."

Alvarez was silent. At least they had the mother's license plate number. He could call it in to his flunkeys at the police department and tell them to be on the lookout for her vehicle.

"You still there?" Hernandez asked.

"Keep your phone on you. We might need your help later."

Alvarez hung up.

Seated next to Zapata in the study, Alvarez looked up at Aguado, who was pacing back and forth in front of a massive picture window, its cherry oak frame shining under the lights of the chandeliers.

"They're gone," said Alvarez. "They took off from the Academy this morning. Ed thinks the mother might have picked them up."

Aguado grumbled under his breath. It wasn't much to go on, but they didn't have many other options. "Get a message out to our contacts in the local and state police agencies.

Give them Rincon's plate number and the description of her car. Tell them the first man to bring them to me gets a ten-thousand-dollar bounty."

At the current exchange rate, ten thousand dollars was nearly a year's salary for many police officers in Mexico. Alvarez knew the bounty would be well received.

"Yes, Jefe."

"In the meantime, I want you two to search the area near the Academy. Maybe the gringo is dumb enough to stick around."

Alvarez nodded obediently, rose from his chair and left the study with Zapata in tow.

---

Officer Julio Leyzaola sat in his police-issued Nissan Tsuru, pointing the radar gun at vehicles as they sped down Federal Highway Fifteen D. The small four-door squad car was white with a thick black stripe running down each side, a five-pointed star painted on the driver and passenger doors. The A/C was on the fritz and the vents spewed lukewarm air, causing beads of sweat to roll down Leyzaola's neck and the back of his shirt.

He didn't feel like working today. He was bored with traffic duty, bored with watching cars whiz past. With each passing vehicle he wondered about its destination. Was the driver going somewhere important? Somewhere interesting? He guessed anywhere would be better than manning his post on this godforsaken stretch of highway.

Leyzaola glanced at the phone attached to his dash as the screen lit up with a message—Miguel Alvarez.

> Looking for a tan Toyota Corolla. Early 2000s model. License plate number VHA-79-20. Bounty is $10,000 US dollars. Mexican woman, approximate age 30. Mexican kid, approximate age 15. White guy, approximate age 30. Detain them and alert me.

Leyzaola stared at the message. He'd done odd jobs for Alvarez here and there, but ten thousand U.S. dollars—that was life-changing money. His thoughts swirled. Maybe he could finally buy a car that didn't belch white smoke when he started it.

He sat up in his seat, suddenly alert and scrutinizing each passing car.

But as the afternoon wore on, Officer Leyzaola began to lose interest in the search. Over the last three hours he'd seen three tan Toyota Corollas, though none with the right plate number. Besides, the end of his shift was quickly approaching, and the chances he'd spot the right one were extremely slim.

As he clicked the switch on the Radar gun to off a tan Corolla sped past his position. He quickly scanned the plate: VHA-79-20. He double-checked the number against the text message on his phone.

It was the car Alvarez was looking for! He could almost smell the reward money.

Leyzaola hurriedly switched on his police lights and mashed the accelerator to the floor. The front wheels spun, spraying dirt and gravel in their wake as the vehicle lurched onto the highway.

The engine whined as the small police cruiser labored to close the distance between it and the Corolla. Leyzaola pulled up close behind the vehicle—three occupants, just like the description said. He smiled. This was going to be the easiest payday of his life.

Seeing the lights behind it, the Corolla slowed and steered to a pullout on the shoulder of the road, stopping before a bridge that spanned a steep gully beneath the highway.

Leyzaola pulled his car behind the Corolla, blocking it in. Typically, he would call in a stop like this, but not today. He opened the driver door with a creak and stepped out into the afternoon sun. His boots crunched on the gravel as he approached the Corolla's driver's side door and knocked on the window.

The woman inside slowly cranked the window down a few inches. "Hola," she said, peeking through the small gap.

"Hola, Señora. Driver's license please."

The woman fumbled in a small bag lying on the console and produced a wallet, from which she removed a worn-looking driver's license.

Leyzaola took the card and examined it. Anna Rincon. "Wait here." He said and returned to his vehicle.

---

Reynolds watched from the side-view mirror as the officer retreated to his car.

"Why did he pull us over?" Reynolds questioned. "Were you speeding?"

"No," Anna replied. "I was going below the speed limit on purpose."

Reynolds didn't like it. Shouldn't the officer at least have explained the reason for pulling them over? He didn't know how it worked in Mexico, but he couldn't shake the feeling that something wasn't right.

He continued watching the officer as he sat in his car.

The cop fumbled with something on the dash, then put a cell phone to his right ear.

*Shouldn't he be using a radio?* Reynolds thought. He'd seen enough cop shows on television to know they always called dispatch with the location of a traffic stop in case something went wrong.

Reynolds' pulse quickened. "Something's wrong," he said, glancing at Anna then back to the mirror.

"What is it?" she asked.

"The cop. He's using a cell phone, not a radio. He's not calling this into the station."

Before Anna could respond, the officer stepped out of his vehicle and returned to the Corolla, this time on the passenger side.

Reynolds eyed the man. He was stocky with a large belly that hung over his duty belt, and his face was dominated by a bushy mustache that clung to his upper lip. His hand rested loosely on his sidearm, and the leather retaining strap dangled free so the weapon could be drawn quickly.

He stared at Reynolds and motioned for him to roll down the window. Before it was halfway down the officer barked, "Señor, please step out of the vehicle. Keep your hands where I can see them."

Reynolds was on high alert. This was more than a garden variety shakedown. There was something wrong here. He shot a quick glance at Anna, then slowly opened the door with his right hand as he held his left in the air.

He swung the door open and stepped out. The air was humid and heavy and smelled of brine.

"Turn around and place your hands on the hood of the vehicle," the officer commanded.

Reynolds complied, his mind racing. He couldn't allow this man to arrest them. This cop was crooked, and he knew it. But what was he going to do? The cop had a gun and who knew what other kind of weaponry. He had to buy some time to think.

Reynolds turned his head as the officer patted down his legs and moved to his torso. "Officer, can I ask why we're being detained?"

The officer grabbed the back of Reynolds' head and slammed it hard on the hood of the Corolla. The impact sent a wave of pain through Reynolds' skull as he tried to keep his eyes open. His vision was suddenly dotted with bright flashes of light, strobing in and out then quickly subsiding.

Anna shrieked inside the vehicle. Danny's eyes went wide with fear.

Bending down, the officer breathed heavily into Reynolds ear. "You will speak when I tell you to. And if you don't cooperate," he slowly licked his lips, "I'll take your woman into the trees with me. Understand?"

Reynolds grunted in the affirmative, his head pounding now, a dull thump echoing in his eardrums.

He should have been terrified. *Should* have. Here he was, stopped on the side of the highway, in the middle of a foreign country, being worked over by a crooked cop.

But instead of fear or panic, a calm sense of determination washed over him. His pulse slowed and the muscles in his forearms flexed and released just as they had before stepping into the batter's box in a tight game.

The officer was short and fat—completely out of shape. He could overpower this buffoon easily enough. Plus, the guy hadn't radioed anything into his station or base or whatever they called it in Mexico. So, there wouldn't be any cavalry coming—at least not for a while.

As the officer finished his pat down, he growled, "Put your hands behind your back."

Reynolds knew it was now or never. His body tensed. He

clenched his fist and cocked his elbow like a hammer, whirling around and smashing a vicious blow into the officer's nose.

The man howled in pain and dropped to his knees as blood gushed from his mashed nasal passages. Reynolds jumped on the stunned officer, straddling his chest, and launched a flurry of cutting elbows into the man's face.

The cop tried to protect himself by covering his head with his arms, but the force of Reynolds' elbows easily broke through the man's guard, pounding his face into a bloody pulp.

The final blow was a vicious right that would've made Chuck Liddell proud. It landed flush on the officer's temple and knocked him out cold.

Reynolds breathed heavy, still atop the motionless police officer. He looked down at the man's battered face then held two fingers to his neck. He was still alive, but he'd wish he was dead when he woke up.

Anna gasped and held her hands over her mouth as Danny stood wide-eyed beside her.

"Oh no!" She sounded terrified. "What did you do?"

Amid the skirmish, Reynolds hadn't heard them approach. He turned, startled, looking up from his position atop the police officer. "Trust me." He squinted into the sun as it formed a halo behind Anna's head. "This guy was bad news."

"You're right," she replied. "But what are we going to do now?"

"Grab his right arm." Reynolds instructed, getting to his feet, and taking hold of the officer's left arm. "Danny, let us know if any cars are coming."

The boy nodded and turned his attention to the road as Reynolds and Anna dragged the officer's limp body over the edge of the gully and down the slope, out of sight from the road.

As Reynolds walked back to the police car, he stopped at the hood where his hands had been and rubbed it with his t-shirt, hopefully wiping away any prints.

"I'm going to move his car so we can get out," he called to Anna, before walking to the driver's side of the police cruiser.

The keys were still in the ignition and the radio crackled something in Spanish. He started the engine. Reynolds looked at the cell phone mounted to the dash. The screen was still unlocked. He clicked the button to bring up recent calls and scanned the list. The very first name was Miguel Alvarez.

Reynolds slammed his fist on the steering wheel. He knew it. The cop was a cartel flunkey.

Reynolds silently cursed the crooked cop and shifted the car in reverse, waiting for Anna to pull the Corolla to the shoulder up ahead. As he shifted into drive, he steered the vehicle to the edge of the ravine and stepped out of the car, allowing it to roll slowly down the embankment and disappear over the side, coming to a stop fifteen feet down the hill.

## CHAPTER 13

"Leyzaola's got them," Alvarez announced. "They're on Highway Fifteen D just north of Tepic. We can be there in a few hours."

"What are you waiting for?" Aguado replied.

Alvarez and Zapata sped down the highway at ninety miles an hour, the Escalade's refined suspension smoothing out the bumps in the neglected asphalt.

"We should be getting close," said Alvarez. "Call Leyzaola and let him know."

Zapata punched in the number for Leyzaola and put the phone to his ear, listening intently. A few seconds passed as he ended the call, then punched in the number again. There was no message, no voicemail. The line just rang and rang.

"He's not answering," Zapata said, glancing at Alvarez.

"Keep trying him. That cabron probably lost them already."

Alvarez did as he was instructed, dialing the number every few minutes for the remainder of the ride.

The Escalade slowed to a stop right before the bridge Leyzaola had described on the phone, but the pullout on the side of the road was empty. Alvarez slammed the gearshift into park and opened the driver door. There were tire tracks everywhere in the dirt. It looked like two vehicles had parked here at some point, but were now gone.

"You think he took them somewhere else?" Zapata asked.

"Why would he?" Alvarez replied. "Something's wrong. Why isn't he answering his phone?"

Alvarez examined the tire tracks. One set led to the shoulder of the road twenty feet ahead of them, and the other...his eyes narrowed. It looked like the tracks went over the side of the ravine.

He walked along the tire tracks, following them to the edge of the ravine and looked over.

Fifteen feet down the embankment, a black and white Nissan police car was wedged among a thicket of Lote Bushes, its emergency lights bathing the foliage in shades of crimson and blue.

Zapata pointed a few feet up the hillside, to their right. "Look there."

A body lay motionless on the embankment. Alvarez skidded down the slope and examined the body. The face was pulverized and unrecognizable, but Alvarez knew it was Leyzaola.

"Dead?" Zapata asked, as Alvarez reached the edge of the ravine.

"He's alive. But he won't be when the coyotes get to him tonight." He spat over the ravine in the direction of Leyzaola's body and began walking back to the SUV. "Stupid cabron."

---

They drove in silence as Reynolds stared out the window, replaying the fight with the cop over and over.

He'd been in a few scraps as a kid, but he'd never really beaten anyone up. Especially a beating as severe as the one he'd just meted out to the dirty cop whose battered body now lay on the side of a ravine.

Reynolds kept assuring himself that he didn't have a choice. The officer was surely going to deliver them to the cartel, and they'd be as good as dead if that happened. He shook the guilt from his head. He'd done what he had to do to protect Anna and Danny—and he'd do it again if necessary.

Up ahead, they approached a lumbering pickup truck.

As Anna slowed the car, waiting for a break in the oncoming traffic to pass, Reynolds examined the vehicle. It was a wobbly old Ford Ranger, overloaded with stacks of bald tires. The piles of rubber stretched above the cab and bulged over the sides of the truck bed, weighing down the rear and causing the pickup to squat low on its rear axle.

Reynolds looked at the plate. It was different from the ones in Mazatlán. He guessed each state had their own design, like back home.

As Anna pressed the accelerator and sped around the truck, Reynolds narrowed his eyes. *The license plate,* he thought. How else could the cop have known it was them? Somehow the cartel had gotten Anna's plate number.

"Your license plate," Reynolds said, breaking the silence in the vehicle. "Must be how that cop spotted us."

Anna remained silent.

"How far are we from Guadalajara?" he asked.

"Another two hours at least," Anna replied. "Why?"

"That's still a long way. And who knows how many other crooked cops are out there looking for us. We need to ditch this license plate fast."

They were on the outskirts of a small town called Tepic,

and Reynolds spotted a service station a few hundred feet ahead on the right.

"Pull into that gas station up ahead. I'm going to get us a new plate."

The station was busy, the lot filled with large trucks, busses and passenger cars fighting for spots at the row of gas pumps in front of the building.

Anna pulled the car off the highway and into the parking lot, where she wove through the swarm of vehicles.

"There," Reynolds said, pointing at an empty parking stall next to a dirty silver sedan. The passenger rear tire was flat and the layer of dust on the windows of the sedan indicated the owner had been gone for a while.

Anna pulled into the empty parking stall and Reynolds stepped out of the car, pulling a fifty-centavo coin from his pocket.

He approached the sedan and knelt at the rear of the vehicle, examining the license plate. It was attached to the vehicle with two flat head screws. One by one, Reynolds put the edge of the coin into the head of each screw and quickly removed them, grabbing the plate and quickly switching it with the one on the Corolla.

"Let's go," he said as Anna eyed him, realizing this was the first time in her life she'd stolen something.

Reynolds read the look on her face. "Sorry, but we need this way more than that guy does right now."

She shrugged and backed the Corolla out of the parking stall, then navigated through the maze of vehicles in the crowded lot.

"Danny, we're just borrowing the license plate," she said, looking into the rearview mirror. "I'll try to find the owner and return it somehow."

In the back seat, Danny rolled his eyes. "I know mom, but like Dillon said, we need it more than he does."

Anna knew he was right, but even now she wouldn't miss a chance to teach her son the difference between right and wrong.

Thanks to the fresh license plate, the rest of the ride to the Consulate was uneventful. Reynolds recounted stories from his playing career and Danny soaked in the tales like a thirsty sponge.

Eventually even Anna opened up, talking about her childhood in Villa Unión, her parents that had passed away years ago and her love for cooking traditional Mexican recipes that had been handed down though her family, generation to generation.

To Reynolds, it almost felt like the road trips his family used to take in their old Suburban. And then his thoughts pulled him back to their precarious reality. The old Suburban had never been in danger of being held up by crooked cops or Mexican gangsters. And his mother and father had never been in possession of a secret drug formula coveted by the cartel.

It was late afternoon when the Corolla rolled to a stop, parking on a side street near the U.S. Consulate building in Guadalajara. Reynolds grabbed his pack from the back seat and removed the envelope, folding it neatly and putting it in his back pocket.

The Consulate took up over half a city block in the heart of the city. Its walls were guarded by a twelve-foot-tall metal fence, covered in green fabric to keep prying eyes from scanning the interior. Dozens of cameras poked out from every angle of the structure and four elevated guard towers dotted each corner of the property.

As they approached a row of service windows toward the end of the building, Reynolds spotted three Mexican police officers. They were armed with AR-15 rifles and stood guarding a sliding gate that led to a parking lot inside the compound.

He stopped and grabbed Anna's arm. "Maybe it would be better if I go to the window alone. An American going to the U.S. Consulate won't raise any eyebrows. Wait for me at the other end of the building and I'll text you when I know something."

"Okay," she said, and turned with Danny down the sidewalk. Looking over her shoulder, she called, "Be careful."

Reynolds didn't say a word, just winked and shot her his trademark smile, then continued to the window.

This late in the evening, only one of the service windows was open, and a woman stood in front of it speaking rapidly and gesturing about something Reynolds couldn't understand.

He waited while the woman kept talking and gesturing, seemingly without taking a breath for the next fifteen minutes. Finally, she nodded, and the agent slid a piece of paper under the glass, apparently satisfying the rapid talker and putting an end to the conversation.

"Next," the agent called through a circular speaker mounted in the center of the glass. "How can I help you, sir?"

The agent was in her mid-fifties, with a pair of thick reading glasses and an equally thick New York accent.

"Sounds like you're a long way from home," Reynolds said, trying to connect with the woman.

"Yeah, lucky me. You take two years of Spanish in junior college, and this is your reward. What can I help you with, sir?"

The agent was clearly in no mood for conversation. Reynolds cleared his throat. "Well, I'm not exactly sure how you can help me."

He launched into a CliffsNotes version of his predicament with the envelope, the cartel and explained Danny and Anna's involvement.

When he'd finished, the agent stared at him, expressionless, over the frames of her reading glasses. "So, you're in possession of a super-secret drug formula and the entire cartel is after you and your friends so they can get it back? And you think we can help you? That about sum it up?"

Reynolds had to admit that, when she phrased it like that, his story did sound a bit ridiculous. "Well yeah, but ..."

He got out three words before she cut him off and shoved a clipboard under the window. "Fill these out to the best of your ability and bring them back to the window when you're done."

Reynolds sighed. This wasn't going at all like he'd imagined. In the movies, distressed Americans ran to the Consulate and uniformed soldiers with M-16 rifles hurriedly admitted them before closing the gates on their pursuers. This place wasn't like that at all. In fact, this place seemed more like a trip to the DMV.

Undeterred, Reynolds quickly filled out the paperwork and returned to the window. The woman looked up as he slid the clipboard under the window, then read through the paperwork. "I'll have to run this by a supervisor to see if we can help you. Wait here."

Reynolds' stomach churned. If his own government couldn't help him ... he didn't even want to think about the possibility. He stepped away from the window and looked down the sidewalk. Anna and Danny were still there, leaning against a concrete planter box that stood between the sidewalk and the road.

"Sir?" Reynolds turned back to the sound of a man's voice coming from an entry door next to the service window.

The man was of medium build with neatly combed

brown hair. He wore dark slacks, and a white-collared shirt with the sleeves rolled up. A Glock nineteen hung from his side.

"I'm agent Frank Henderson with the DEA. I understand you're in some trouble."

"A little bit," Reynolds quipped.

"Why don't you step inside so we can talk?"

Reynolds nodded. "There are two other people involved here. Can they come in as well?"

"Yes, I'll need statements from each of you."

Reynolds quickly pulled the phone from his pocket and texted Anna to meet him at the entrance.

When Anna and Danny arrived, Agent Henderson stepped out and held the door. "Come inside," he said.

The entry was stark, and coated in a pale yellow hue under the glare of the fluorescent bulbs. The floors were made from large squares of polished aggregate, and the walls were painted a shade of uniquely bureaucratic cream.

Henderson led the group through a metal detector and down a hallway into a small office. The office was crammed with a large cherry-colored wooden desk, a high-backed office chair, two guest chairs and a black leather sofa.

Henderson motioned for the group to take a seat.

"So," he said. "Tell me what's going on."

―――――

Alvarez and Zapata sat quietly in the Escalade, mulling their next move. The gringo had done a number on Leyzaola. And while Alvarez knew Leyzaola was a fool, he was still a police officer. If the gringo was willing to beat the hell out of a cop like that, then he was desperate, which made him dangerous.

To make matters worse, now the group knew they were

being tracked. Unless they were complete morons, they would switch vehicles, hop on a bus, or hunker down somewhere. Chances were they'd never find the little Corolla again.

Alvarez ran a hand over his perfectly slicked back hair. He hated returning to Aguado with bad news, but it might be necessary. Right now, they were at a dead end.

As Alvarez chewed on the problem, Zapata scrolled through an email on his phone. It was from another police officer on the cartel's payroll. Attached to the email was a file titled *Background Screening Summary*.

Zapata clicked on the attachment and began reading.

- Anna Rincon
- Thirty years old.
- Address: Margarita Maza de Juárez 202, Villa Unión, Sinaloa, Mexico
- Divorced. Ex-husband, Juan Luis Rincon of Guadalajara, Jalisco, Mexico.
- One child, Daniel Antonio Rincon.
- Both parents deceased.
- No siblings.
- Employed by the Casa Royale Resort in Mazatlán.
- No criminal history.

"What's that?" Alvarez asked.

Zapata handed him the phone. "Background check on the woman. One of our guys in Sinaloa sent it over."

Alvarez read through the report. Nothing useful.

He went to hand the phone back to Zapata, then stopped and scrolled back to the top of the attachment. *What about the ex-husband?* he thought. *Maybe he could be useful.*

Alvarez had never been married, and thus had never been divorced. But he'd seen other men go through the process and it almost always ended with each spouse despising the other. What if the woman didn't want to talk to the ex-husband?

But that still left the kid. Maybe this Juan guy still had a relationship with his son. Maybe he could persuade the boy to meet him somewhere.

Alvarez decided it was worth a shot. Besides, they didn't have any other options right now.

He shifted the Escalade into drive and looked at Zapata. "Let's pay the ex-husband a visit."

## CHAPTER 14

Agent Henderson listened patiently for the better part of an hour, taking statements from Reynolds, Anna, and Danny. He jotted notes on a yellow legal pad and underlined the parts Reynolds assumed were most important.

"This is quite a predicament you've found yourself in," he said, and scribbled one last note before setting down the ball-point pen. "Tell me again about this Felix Martin. The guy that crashed into your table at dinner."

Reynolds recounted the evening at the restaurant, and went over the letter Martin had dropped along with the thumb drive.

"And do you have the envelope with you?"

Reynolds shook his head. "No, I stashed it in a safe deposit box at my bank," he lied.

Anna shot him a sideways glance, but Reynolds didn't react. If he'd learned one thing over the last twenty-four hours, it was to trust no one, not even the DEA.

Henderson grunted and jotted another note on the pad.

"Do you have any idea where this Felix Martin might be?" he asked.

"No," Reynolds replied. "The last time we saw him he was being chased down an alley by two guys with guns. For all we know they kidnapped or killed him."

"How about the drugs? Did you actually see them being manufactured?"

"No," Reynolds replied.

How about Aguado or Alvarez? Did you personally witness either of them committing a crime?"

Reynolds could feel the conversation going sideways. "Well, no, we didn't."

Henderson's expression softened, and he leaned back in his chair exhaling deeply. "Listen, I believe your story. We've known about Aguado and Alvarez for a long time—and you're right, they're very bad guys. I'd love nothing more than to put those two behind bars. But unless we have rock solid proof, there's not a lot the DEA can do. It's hard enough to get arrest warrants in the States, but down here? You better have a smoking gun."

Reynolds' shoulders slumped, and Danny dropped his gaze to the floor.

Henderson continued, "If we had Felix Martin, someone with direct ties to Aguado, someone who could testify against him, then we could do something. But everything you have is hearsay."

"But what about the letter and the drive?" Reynolds shot back.

"That letter could have been written by anyone," Henderson replied. "And the drive? We can look at it, but the wheels of the DEA turn slowly. And since we're on foreign soil, they turn even slower. We could be looking at weeks or months for our analysts to examine a random computer drive from an unvetted source."

Reynolds tilted his head toward the ceiling and closed

his eyes, shielding them from the harsh glow of the fluorescent bulbs. "So, you're saying there's nothing you can do. We just take our chances and try to hide from the cartel for the rest of our lives?"

"I'm not saying that at all Mr. Reynolds. If you'd like, I can try to expedite an emergency visa for Ms. Rincon and Danny. It usually takes three to five weeks, but I can try to push it through faster. From there, we can help all of you get a flight to the States."

Reynolds looked at Anna. "What do you think?"

"I think it's our only option," she replied.

"Good." Henderson opened a drawer underneath his desk and removed a handful of paperwork. "I'll need you to fill out one of these forms for yourself Ms. Rincon and one for Danny. Then I'll just need a copy of your driver's license and Danny's birth certificate."

Anna's face went pale. Her driver's license. The crooked cop on the highway had never returned it. Her ID was probably still in the bottom of the ravine with the police car.

Not to mention she hadn't even thought to bring Danny's birth certificate with her. In fact, she'd been so frazzled by the break in she hadn't brought anything with her.

Anna grabbed Reynolds' knee and squeezed hard as if saying trust me. "I'm afraid we don't have our identification with us, Agent Henderson."

Reynolds looked at her surprised, then remembered. He'd forgotten to get her license out of the cop car. *Shit!* If the police found her ID in the car, then the crooked cops *and* the legitimate ones would be searching for them.

"Without proper identification," Henderson said, "I can't even start the process."

Things had just gone from bad to worse.

Reynolds leaned forward. "Agent Henderson, we'll head

back to Villa Unión right now and get their IDs. Can we come back tomorrow?"

"I'll be here all day tomorrow," Henderson replied, and slid two business cards across the desk, one to Reynolds and the other to Anna. "In the meantime, if you remember something else that could help us, please give me a call—day or night."

The group rose from their chairs and Reynolds stuck out his hand. "Thanks for at least hearing us out, Agent Henderson."

The agent returned the handshake and escorted the group from the office and back down the hallway to the front door of the Consulate.

Outside, they walked in silence back to the car. When they sat down in the little Corolla, Reynolds fixed a solemn gaze on Anna. "We have to get your license out of that cop car—tonight."

Tears began streaming down her cheeks as she reached to put the key in the ignition. Reynolds put a hand on her arm and pulled it away from the steering column. "We're going to figure something out, Anna. There's a good chance they haven't found the police car yet, and we can just go back and get your ID."

"But what if they've found it already? I'll go to prison for sure." She replied, wiping away the tears. And Danny's birth certificate—it's back at the apartment. You know we can't go back there."

Reynolds agreed, but tried to assure her. "We'll cross that bridge when we come to it. Let's just focus on getting your ID first."

Anna forced a smile and turned the key in the ignition. "Okay, thank you, Dillon."

Again, he simply winked and flashed her his trademark smile.

She grinned, genuinely this time, and pulled the vehicle onto the street.

———

After driving five hours south from Mazatlán to Tepic, it had taken another two hours to reach Guadalajara where Juan Rincon lived. It was getting late and both Alvarez and Zapata were itching to get out of the SUV and stretch their legs.

During the drive, Zapata had made a couple of calls and gotten an address for Juan. He lived in a notoriously dangerous area of the city called Colonia Jalisco, a small neighborhood on the east side of Guadalajara.

Alvarez knew they had to be careful here. The state of Jalisco was teeming with members of the Jalisco New Generation Cartel, or the CJNG.

The CJNG had once been a powerful ally of the Sinaloa cartel, but in 2017 the CJNG broke the alliance and the rival factions had been at war ever since. Any CJNG foot soldier that put a bullet in either Alvarez or Zapata would be hailed as a hero, so they had to proceed cautiously.

The sidewalks of Colonia Jalisco were littered with dusty piles of construction debris and bags of rotting trash. The buildings were all in various stages of decay, with crumbling walls, overgrown courtyards and boarded-up windows. Juan's house was a particularly good example of just how decrepit the neighborhood had become.

It was a narrow stucco shack, painted lime green with rusty barred windows. The exterior of the property was lined with a crudely erected fence made from empty plastic milk crates, stacked three layers high. The gate was fashioned from two weathered pallets scabbed together and nailed to a rickety wooden post.

A small white pickup truck took up most of the front yard, which was covered by a makeshift awning made of ragged tarps tied together and strung between the house and a large tree in the front.

Alvarez opened the flimsy gate and stepped into the front yard, Zapata following behind. As they approached the front door, a small chihuahua began barking incessantly and nipped at Alvarez's pant leg before he kicked the tiny dog, sending it yelping away down the side of the house.

Alvarez knocked on the door loudly. "Mr. Rincon," he demanded.

No answer.

Zapata peered through the single window in the front of the house—no light, no movement inside.

"He's not there," said a voice.

Alvarez swung his head in the direction of the voice. An old man sat on a plastic lawn chair in the neighboring yard, staring into the darkness.

"He's at the Alamo this time of night," the voice continued.

Alvarez picked his way through the weeds and around the white pickup truck. "What's the Alamo?" he asked over the fence.

"It's a bar. About ten minutes from here. He goes there every night."

Without a word, Alvarez and Zapata returned to the SUV. They didn't have time to wait for this drunk to stumble his way home from the bar. They'd have to go find him.

Ten minutes later, Alvarez pulled the Escalade into the lone empty parking spot in the lot and stepped out.

The bars in this part of town were notoriously rough, but this one was a first-class shithole. Its gray and blue painted walls were missing huge chunks of plaster, and the three orange doors that dotted the front of the building were crudely spray painted with the hours of operation and various promotions for drink specials.

The building featured a parapet in the center of the scalloped roofline, presumably to give the appearance of the real Alamo, but this building's façade was lined with rolls of razor wire. For what purpose, Alvarez didn't care to know.

Every head inside the bar turned when Alvarez and Zapata entered. Thankfully, it was dark, lit only by a couple of dim overhead lights and a few strands of neon tubing haphazardly placed along the paint-peeling walls. Cigarette smoke hung thick in the air, and the soles of Alvarez's boots stuck to the floor, making a scratchy, Velcro-like sound as he walked towards the bar.

Behind the counter, a greasy-looking man in a tank top stood washing a glass, towel over his shoulder. "What can I get you?" he asked, clenching a tiny stub of cigar between his teeth.

"I'm looking for Juan Rincon," Alvarez replied.

The bartender stopped fussing with the glass and stared at Alvarez. "I asked what you wanted to drink, cabron."

Alvarez looked at Zapata, then around the bar. They were outnumbered ten to one in here, and as much as he despised it, diplomacy seemed the best course of action right now. "Two Pacificos."

The bartender pulled two hazy beer mugs from beneath the counter and filled them from a worn tap until foam spilled over the sides. "Sixty pesos," the man said, and sat the mugs on the bar top.

Alvarez slid a hundred-dollar bill across the bar. "Juan Rincon."

The bartender flicked his head to the corner of the room, where a slight man in his thirties sat at a wooden table with a chubby woman, whose sheer dress was at least two sizes two small. The man wore a black t-shirt over baggy blue jeans that hung off his skinny frame. A few days-worth of stubble covered his features and there was a poorly-drawn rose tattooed on the side of his neck.

Alvarez and Zapata threaded their way through the tables to the corner where Juan was seated.

"Juan Rincon?" Alvarez asked.

"Yeah. Who's asking?"

"I have a business proposition for you," Alvarez said and discreetly flashed a roll of hundred-dollar bills.

Rincon straightened in his chair.

"Beat it," Alvarez barked at the chubby woman.

The woman looked at Juan for help, but without hesitation, he nodded for her to leave.

Reluctantly, she did as she was told, grabbing her purse and walking from the table, leaving a string of profanity in her wake.

"Are you in contact with your ex-wife, Anna Rincon?" Alvarez asked.

"I haven't talked to that bitch in years," Rincon replied, and took a shot of tequila.

"What about your son, Danny?"

Rincon just held up his hands and shrugged, his face apathetic.

"I need you to contact her."

"Why?"

"We want to talk to her and your son in person. That's all you need to know."

"What's in it for me?" Juan asked, eying Alvarez suspiciously.

"Five thousand U.S. dollars."

They had Juan's full attention now. "What if I get ahold of her? What do you want me to say?" he asked.

"Tell her you want to see Danny."

"I haven't seen Danny in years," Juan scoffed. "She'll never believe that."

Alvarez wasn't a patient man. When he offered someone five thousand dollars, he expected them to bring something to the table. He leaned close to Juan and growled through gritted teeth. "Then make up something she *will* believe."

Juan was a lot of things. Abusive husband, absentee father, career alcoholic. But he wasn't completely obtuse. He knew these men were serious and would probably kill him if he didn't figure something out. Plus, the five grand would be a nice payday.

"Okay, okay, I'll think of something," he thought for a moment, before a sleazy smile crept over his face. "I've got it."

He dialed Anna's number. The line rang five times, then went to voicemail.

"No answer," Juan said, looking to Alvarez.

"Try again."

Juan dialed the number again but got the same result. "I got a new phone. She probably won't recognize the number."

"Then text her," Alvarez ordered.

Juan sloppily moved his fingers over the keyboard and hit send. The message read:

> Anna, it's Juan. I've become very ill, and I don't know how much longer I have left. I would like to see Danny before it's too late. Please call me.

They waited for ten minutes in awkward silence, each staring at the phone as if willing it to ring. Finally, Juan said, "She's probably asleep."

Alvarez thought about this for a moment. "We'll be at

your house tomorrow morning at nine. You can try her again, then."

Without another word, Alvarez and Zapata walked out of the bar into the night. Juan wondered what the men wanted with his ex-wife and son. What had they done? He shrugged and took another shot. "Who cares?" he muttered, "I'll be five thousand bucks richer tomorrow."

# CHAPTER 15

The little Corolla sped down Federal Highway Fifteen D, keeping close to the posted speed limit. Anna was tired from all the driving. It had been over seven hours to get from Mazatlán to Guadalajara, and now they'd driven another two and a half hours to reach the outskirts of Tepic.

Reynolds remembered the ravine with the police car was a few miles north of the city, but in the dark it was hard to pinpoint the exact location.

"Slow down a little," he said to her. "I think we're getting close."

He scanned the dark landscape through Anna's window. Thick foliage whirred past, lit only by the waning half-moon.

"Stop here. I see the bridge."

To their left was a galvanized steel guard rail, lining the far side of the bridge. At its end was the dirt pullout where they'd parked earlier in the day. It was empty. No swarm of cop cars, no hordes of police officers—nothing.

He wondered if the police had come and gone already. Had they been here earlier and retrieved both the vehicle and their injured officer? Reynolds remembered the lights of the cop car were still on when he sent it into the ravine, but now there was only darkness.

He took a deep breath. *Only one way to find out.*

"Pull into the turnout and shut off the lights—but leave the car running. We might need to get out of here quick."

Anna pulled the car across the highway onto the dirt patch behind the guardrail and turned off the Corolla's headlights.

"Stay here," Reynolds instructed. "I'm going to go check things out. Honk twice if there's a problem."

Reynolds quickly jogged to the edge of the ravine and peered down. It was dark, but in the dim moonlight, he could barely make out the silhouette of the police car resting at the bottom. The lights must have drained the battery and faded out before it got dark.

*Lucky.*

Next, he scanned the area where he and Anna had dragged the cop down the embankment. His body was still there. Reynolds wondered if the cop was still alive, but quickly shelved his concern, remembering how the man had threatened Anna. Yeah, he could stay there forever as far as Reynolds cared.

He picked his way down the embankment, carefully placing each step on the large chunks of rock that jutted out of the hillside. He didn't dare use the light on his phone, fearing that a passing motorist would see him and stop, so the going was slow.

Finally, Reynolds reached the police car and opened the driver's side door. He clicked on his phone light and panned around the interior of the vehicle. The car was filthy and littered with crumpled up fast food wrappers and empty soda cans. This guy was a real pig.

As Reynolds continued scanning the interior, he shone the light on the floorboards, starting on the passenger side, then moving to the driver's side. As he stared into the pile of rubbish, a piece of white plastic glinted in the light. Reynolds quickly plucked it from beneath a half-eaten bag of French fries and examined the card—it was Anna's driver's license.

He exhaled a sigh of relief and carefully shut the door, wiping his prints from the handle before clicking off his phone light.

Reynolds slowly summited the embankment and dusted himself off before approaching the car, startling both Anna and Danny when he opened the door.

"Got it." With a smile, he handed the ID to Anna.

Relief washed over her as she took the license, hands trembling. "Thank you, thank you, thank you," she said, and kissed the plastic card before returning it to her wallet.

Reynolds looked at her. "Now all we need is Danny's birth certificate."

---

The group was exhausted. By the time they had retrieved Anna's driver's license, it was late, and they needed rest. Anna steered the little car back to Tepic, where Reynolds paid cash for a dingy hotel room with two queen beds and a fuzzy television that only received two channels, both airing soccer games.

Reynolds and Danny sprawled out on the beds while Anna took a shower. It was the first time he and Danny had a minute to really talk since the previous day.

"You okay, kiddo?" Reynolds asked.

Danny took a huge bite from a hamburger they'd gotten at a fast-food place around the corner. "I'm okay," he said, barely able to speak through the mouthful of food. "But that's cop's toast. How'd you learn to fight like that?"

Reynolds smiled and shook his head as he poked through a paper bag filled with French fries. "I don't know. First time I've ever been in a fight like that before."

"Didn't look like it," Danny said, jumping off the bed and throwing elbows and fists into the air. "Looked like you belong in the octagon."

Reynolds chuckled. "Yeah, maybe I'll do that from now on. Couldn't be any more dangerous than this." He pointed to the scar under his left eye and made a funny face.

They both laughed and continued joking until Anna stepped out of the bathroom.

"What's so funny out here?" she said, trying to contain a smile of her own.

"I was just telling Dillon he should try out for the UFC," Danny said, again throwing punches into the air.

Anna shot a look of disapproval at Reynolds, who simply held up his palms and shrugged.

She returned her attention to Danny. "Fighting is never the answer, Mijo. Violence doesn't solve anything."

"Sure solved our problem with that cop today," Danny said, and burst out laughing. Reynolds couldn't help but join him, and eventually even Anna cracked a half-smile.

"You two," she said. "Always full of jokes."

The group quickly finished the remainder of their late-night dinner and climbed into bed, exhausted.

Reynolds' sleep came in spurts, and he woke every couple of hours to look out the window or double check the deadbolt. But even the troubled sleep was welcome. His head still ached from being smashed on the hood of the car, and the snippets of rest helped.

The next morning, sun filtered through gaps in the curtains, projecting shafts of light along the walls and across the beds.

Reynolds opened his eyes. His head still hurt from the

day before, but not nearly as much. He stretched his arms and sat up against the wobbly headboard.

"Morning," he said, seeing Anna seated on the edge of the bed studying her phone while Danny slept in the next bed.

"I'm going downstairs to get some coffee," she whispered. "Would you like to come with me?"

Reynolds rubbed his eyes. "Yeah, give me a couple of minutes to get dressed."

He hurriedly pulled on the same jeans he'd worn the day before and changed into a fresh t-shirt, then laced up his shoes and stood near the door. "Ready?"

Anna nodded. The pair quietly slipped out of the hotel room, locking the door behind them.

As they descended the stairs to the lobby Anna said, "Dillon, last night when we were asleep, Danny's father called twice. Then he texted me. He said he was ill and wanted to see Danny."

"Do you really think he's telling the truth?" Reynolds asked.

"I don't know. I haven't spoken to him in years."

"What about Danny?" Reynolds pressed. "Does he talk to his dad often?"

Anna shook her head. "Never. Juan has never even tried to see Danny since we left."

"Are you going to call him back?" Reynolds asked.

"I don't know. What do you think I should do?"

Reynolds' bullshit detector was now in overdrive.

They entered a small convenience store next to the hotel and he began pouring two cups of coffee from a stainless-steel urn at the rear of the store. "I'm not sure," he said diplomatically. "The timing sure seems odd."

She looked at him and nodded. "I agree. But what if he's

telling the truth? I would feel terrible if I took away Danny's last chance to see his father."

Reynolds grumbled. He still wasn't buying it.

"I know," Anna said. "But I've always felt guilty that Danny never got the chance to have a father in his life. I made the decision to leave Juan and Danny's the one that's had to live with it."

"You're an amazing mother, Anna. I'm sure there was a good reason you left."

*Yes, there was a very good reason I left,* Anna thought as she stared into the cup of steaming coffee.

Reynolds remained leery, but it wasn't like he could stop her. Besides, the guy was Danny's dad. Even if he was a deadbeat, he wouldn't do anything to hurt Danny. Right? He kept telling himself that over and over on the walk back to the hotel room, wanting to believe it was the truth though inwardly doubting it was.

As they reached the room, Reynolds pulled a large brass key from his pocket and turned it in the lock. As he cracked the door open, Anna's phone began ringing. She looked at the screen. It was the same number as last night—Juan.

"I'm going to take this," Anna said. "I'll only be a minute."

---

Agent Henderson stood over a ancient black coffeemaker in the break room of the DEA field office, pouring lumpy powdered creamer into his mug. The room was stark, like the rest of the building—harsh fluorescent lights, plain white cabinets and a tan laminate countertop that was chipping badly at the edges.

"Morning, Frank," called a voice behind him.

Henderson turned to see Benjamin Wilson, a plucky

young analyst that had worked in the Guadalajara office just shy of a year.

"Morning, Ben," Henderson replied. "I didn't know you were working today."

There were only a handful of agents stationed at this office, and everyone pretty much knew each other's schedule.

"Wasn't supposed to, but Byrnes called in sick last night. Bad chili relleno I guess."

Henderson laughed and sat down at a small bistro table in the corner of the room.

"Anything interesting in your world today?" Wilson asked, taking his turn at the coffeemaker.

Henderson shrugged. "Nah. The usual." Then he remembered the interaction with Reynolds. "Actually, I did have an interesting conversation yesterday."

"With whom?" Wilson asked.

"An American guy traveling with a Mexican woman and her son. They claimed to have gotten their hands on a USB drive that contains some kind of formula for a new street drug that can't be detected by our agents."

Wilson looked over his shoulder skeptically. "Oh yeah? I bet they're really popular with the cartel if they have something like that."

"Yeah, that's the problem. They said the cartel is after them to get it back."

"What did you tell them?" Wilson pressed.

"I told them there's not much we can do. I offered to help with an expedited visa, but the woman didn't have any ID."

"That's convenient," Wilson quipped. "Did they show you the drive?"

"The guy said it was in a safe deposit box at his bank."

"Well, that's convenient too."

"I know, I know. It sounds far-fetched," Henderson

continued. "But I've been doing this a long time and I think there's something to their story. They even mentioned Aguado and Alvarez by name."

Wilson turned from the coffeemaker and raised an eyebrow. "Seriously? They came in off the street with this nonsense and you believed them? Aguado's name is always on the local news. They don't need to be geniuses to figure that out."

"Yeah, there was just something about them, though." Henderson took another sip of his coffee, mulling over the previous day's interaction.

"It'd sure be nice if it was true," Wilson said. "I could do a number on the cartel if we could switch out that drive."

"What do you mean?" Henderson asked.

"I mean, I could install a virus on an identical USB drive that would infect whatever network it was connected to. I could program it to give us full access to their files, contacts, banking information—everything."

"You can do that?" Henderson asked.

"Why do you think the DEA hired me? I have skiiiiilllls." He purposely drew out the word and burst into a terrible version of "The Dougie."

Henderson stared blankly at the young agent as he bopped around the break room. *This generation will be running the country someday. God help us.*

"You finished?" Henderson asked flatly.

Wilson stopped dancing. "I was just getting warmed up."

If that was the warmup, Henderson most definitely did not want to see the grand finale. "You were serious about the USB drive, though? You can really do that?"

"Yeah," Wilson replied. "I've already got most of it programmed for another case. The hard part is going to be convincing Aguado or someone else on the network to plug it into their computer."

"You let me worry about that part," Henderson said. "How long will it take you to finish the virus?"

"A few hours at most," Wilson replied. "I can have it done this afternoon."

"Alright then, let's see what kind of *skiiiiilllls* you really have," Henderson said mockingly, then quickly strode from the break room before Wilson could burst into another impromptu dance session.

---

The pounding on the front door mirrored the pounding in Juan Rincon's head. The notion of an extra five thousand dollars in his pocket had put him in a good mood the previous night, and he'd indulged a few too many tequila shots.

"Hold on!" he yelled. "I'm coming."

Juan rolled off the couch, still wearing the smoke-saturated clothing from the previous evening. He staggered toward the door and looked out the small window beside it. The men from the bar were back.

The pounding on the door continued, louder now that he was nearer, and Juan winced with each thud, cursing the men under his breath.

He opened the door, allowing Alvarez and Zapata to barge past him and into the living room of the small house.

"We've been banging on the door for ten minutes," Alvarez growled.

"Sorry, I forgot to set an alarm."

Alvarez looked at the disheveled man in disgust. He stunk of smoke, sweat and booze and had clearly slept in the clothes he'd been wearing the night before. His hair was matted on one side and the corners of his mouth were coated in a flaky white crust.

"Make the call," Alvarez said. "Try to find out where she is."

"We're not real friendly," Juan replied. "What if she won't tell me?"

"Then get her to meet you somewhere. The fewer people, the better."

"C'mon man. If she still lives in Villa Unión, that's going to be a long drive. I've got shit to do today."

Zapata stepped forward and threw a vicious right hook into Juan's side. The man doubled over, then dropped to one knee, heaving and gasping to regain his breath.

As he struggled, Alvarez bent down and hissed in his ear. "*This* is what you're doing today, cabron."

"Okay, okay." Juan groaned and staggered to his feet. "Let me get my phone."

Still holding his burning side, Juan slowly shuffled to an end table covered in empty beer cans. Amid the refuse, he retrieved his cell phone and began to dial.

"Put it on speaker," Alvarez directed.

Juan clicked the speaker icon on the screen as the call connected. "Hola Anna, it's Juan." He tried to make his voice sound weak and sickly, but between the wicked hangover and the searing pain in his side, he didn't need to act much.

"Hello Juan," said a soft female voice.

"Anna, I know it's been a long time, but I'm calling because I have leukemia—it's terminal." He had no idea what leukemia was, but he'd heard it somewhere—maybe a movie or a TV show, and it sounded believable enough. "I don't have a lot of time left, and I'd really like to see my son before …" He let his voice trail off in dramatic fashion.

"I'm not sure Juan. We're very busy right now, and I'm not even sure if Danny wants to see you."

"Could you please ask him? I can meet you in Villa Unión this afternoon."

"We're not in Villa Unión," Anna replied.

"Where are you then?" Juan asked.

"We're visiting a friend in Guadalajara."

Juan's eyes went wide as Alvarez and Zapata exchanged glances, silently thanking the Virgin Mary for their good fortune.

"That's perfect." Juan spat out and began unwittingly scratching at the rose tattoo on his neck. "I live here in Guadalajara now. I could come see Danny this afternoon."

The line went quiet for a minute, then the woman's voice returned. "I'll have to ask him if he wants to see you. Let me call you back in a few minutes."

"Ok, thank you, Anna."

The line went dead, and Juan looked at Alvarez. "Tell me again what you want with Anna and the kid?"

Alvarez didn't want this fool getting sentimental on him now. "We just want to talk to them."

The answer seemed to satisfy Juan's curiosity, and he turned his attention to an open bag of pork rinds on the end table.

A few minutes later, the screen on Juan's phone lit up. It was Anna. He quickly gulped down the last of the pork rinds and wiped a greasy hand across his lips, causing crumbs to fall onto the already-filthy carpet below.

"Hola, Anna." He pressed the speaker icon.

"Hola, Juan. I talked to Danny, and he agreed to see you."

Juan flashed a smarmy smile at Alvarez. "That's great. Give me your address. I can be there around ..." He looked at Alvarez for direction.

Alvarez knew they would need to recon the location where the woman was staying, so they'd need a few hours to prepare before the meetup. He held up two fingers.

"I can be there around two o'clock."

"That's fine, but I'd like to meet in a public place," Anna replied.

Juan grimaced. "Are you sure? It's no problem for me to come to you."

"Yes, I'm sure. We can meet at the Gran Terraza this afternoon for lunch."

Alvarez shook his head and mouthed "No," at Juan. "I really don't like to be around a lot of people in my condition. Can we meet somewhere a little more private?"

"I'm sorry, Juan. Either we meet there, or I'm afraid you won't be able to see Danny."

"Um ... let me see how far that is from my house." Juan said, trying to buy some time.

Alvarez could hear the conviction in the woman's voice and knew there would be no talking her out of this. They'd have to meet them at the mall. He sighed and looked at Juan, giving him a reluctant nod.

"Um, okay. Yeah, that will work," Juan said. "I'll meet you at the Gran Terraza at two o'clock this afternoon. Thank you, Anna."

Again, the line went dead, and Juan reached for a half empty beer can. "Now what?"

# CHAPTER 16

Reynolds closed the hotel room door quietly, so as to not disturb Danny. He set his cup of coffee on the nightstand and began thumbing through his phone, trying to figure out where they could get a certified copy of Danny's birth certificate.

As he scrolled through the search results, a message popped open at the top of the screen.

> Dillon, it's Agent Frank Henderson. I was speaking to one of my colleagues here at the office and I think we have an idea that could help both of us out. I've got a few details to work on this morning, but can you meet me here at the Consulate after lunch to discuss?

Reynolds stared at the screen. "... an idea that could help both of us out." He wondered exactly what that meant.

Fortunately, they had some time to kill. His Google search had revealed they could request a duplicate birth certificate at the Civil Registry in Guadalajara, but the office was only open Monday through Friday. Today being Sunday, they would have to wait until tomorrow morning.

Reynolds quickly typed a reply.

> Yes, we can meet you this afternoon. Does 2:00 work?

The response came instantly.

> That works great. See you then.

At least they wouldn't have to sit in this dumpy hotel room and watch fuzzy soccer matches all day.

Reynolds looked up from the phone at the sound of the doorknob turning. Anna poked her head through the door and motioned for him to come out into the hallway.

The corridor was painted sea-foam green and smelled like old food and even older cigarette smoke. Anna leaned against the wall opposite their room, holding her phone when Reynolds emerged.

"It was Juan. He sounds sincere."

Reynolds bit his tongue. "Okay, so are you going to let him see Danny?"

"I told him it was up to Danny, and that I would have to ask him."

Behind Reynolds, the door to the hotel room swung open and Danny stepped out of the dimly lit room, squinting against the lights in the hallway. "What are you guys doing?"

"Just talking, Mijo," Anna replied. "Did you sleep well?"

"Yeah." He yawned. "I'm hungry though."

The kid was an eating machine. It was all Anna could do to keep him fed without sending them to the poorhouse.

"What sounds good?" She asked.

Danny's face turned into a wide smile. "Pizza," he said, making a circular motion around his belly.

"For breakfast?" Anna chided.

"I think I saw a pizza place up the street," Reynolds cut in. "I'm pretty hungry too."

"You two." She looked at Reynolds, then back at Danny. "All right then. Pizza it is." She paused. "Danny, there's something else I wanted to talk to you about."

"What?" He replied impatiently. With pizza on his mind, Danny wasn't in the mood for more conversation.

"It's about your father."

He furrowed his brow, causing his eyebrows to pinch inward and his eyes to narrow.

Anna continued, "I know you haven't seen him since you were a baby, but he's very sick and he wants to see you."

The trio sat in silence for a moment while Danny digested the information. His mother hadn't talked much about his father. He could probably count the number of times on one hand his father's name had been uttered in their house.

But in the back of his mind, he'd always wondered about the man. What did he look like? What did he do for a living? Was he fat? Skinny? Tall? Short?

He had a million more questions, and now they all swirled in his head. "When?" was all he could muster in response.

"Possibly this afternoon." Anna replied. "And Mijo, if you don't want to see him, you don't have to. I told your father it was your choice and if you said no, that would be the end of it."

Somewhere around the corner, a door slammed and Danny stared blankly down the hallway, still thinking. Finally, he turned back to his mother. "Yeah, I guess I want to see him."

"Are you sure?" Anna asked.

"Yeah," Danny replied.

"Ok then. I'll tell him we'll meet this afternoon." Anna looked at Reynolds, knowing his concern.

"Can we go get some pizza now?" Danny pressed.

"Yes," Anna said. "Why don't you go get dressed so I can finish talking with Dillon?"

Danny turned and closed the door to the hotel room behind him.

"I'm sorry," Anna said. "But I have to do this for Danny."

"It's okay," Reynolds replied. "Just make sure we can meet him in a public place."

"We?" she asked.

"You don't think I'm letting you go alone, do you?"

"I appreciate the offer, Dillon, but I can handle this," she replied in a soft yet firm voice.

"Are you absolutely certain?" Reynolds pressed.

"Yes. Plus, the three of us probably shouldn't be spotted together right now."

Reynolds couldn't help but agree. "Okay. I'll stay here."

Anna dialed Juan's number. When the call was over, she looked at Reynolds. "He wants to meet at the mall at two o'clock."

"Ugh, that's going to be a problem."

Anna looked confused. "Why?"

"Because Agent Henderson texted me this morning. He said he might be able to help us, so I told him we'd be at his office at two o'clock this afternoon to talk."

"Can we meet him later? After Danny sees his father?"

"This is too important, Anna. If Henderson has a way out of this mess, I think we should hear him out."

Anna knew he was right. But as much as she wanted to back out of taking Danny to see Juan, she also knew it was probably the last chance he would ever have to see his father. She couldn't take that from him.

"I have to do this, Dillon. Danny may never have a

chance to see his father again. I hope you can understand that."

He was torn. Reynolds thought about his own father. If his dad was on his deathbed, of course he'd want to see him one last time. But the meeting with Henderson was too important to miss. If the agent had a way out of this, Reynolds wanted to know what it was.

"I understand." Reynolds sighed. He could sense Anna wasn't going to budge on the issue. "Why don't we do both? You can drop me off at the Consulate to meet with Henderson, then you and Danny can go see Juan at the mall and come back to get me when you're done. Hopefully, I'll have some answers by then."

Anna thought for a moment. "Yes, I think that should work."

Reynolds smiled wide. "Good, now can we go get some pizza?" And made a circular motion around his belly.

---

Agent Henderson had worked furiously all morning, and now he finally had the framework of a plan blocked out on the screen in front of him—all except for one gaping hole. How were they going to get the drive into Aguado's hands without raising suspicion?

It wasn't like they could call the drug lord's cell phone and tell him to come pick up the drive at the lost and found. *No*, Henderson thought, he had to figure out a way to make Aguado think he had gotten the drive back on his own. It was the only way.

As he stared at the computer, Henderson twirled a pen between his fingers, trying to figure out a solution. Looking up from the screen, his concentration was immediately broken at the sight of Ben Wilson moonwalking into his office, sliding his feet, heel to toe, over the thin carpet. When the young agent had reached Henderson's desk, he faced forward and did the wave with his arms, starting from right to left, finishing the move by holding up a small USB drive between his thumb and index finger.

"Voilà," he said triumphantly, beaming at the tiny piece of hardware in his hand.

Henderson wasn't sure what he'd just witnessed, but he knew he never wanted to see it again. "I guess that means you're done programming the virus?"

"What you're looking at is an advanced piece of technology created by a truly advanced DEA Agent. This little beauty is one hundred percent guaranteed to ruin your neighborhood drug dealer's day—or your money back." He used his best infomercial voice. "Wanna see what this baby can do?"

"I'm giddy with anticipation," Henderson deadpanned.

"I'll need to conduct the demonstration over lunch, your treat, of course," Wilson said.

"Of course. How could I refuse an offer like that?"

The pair walked across the street to a hole-in-the-wall Greek café. Although it was run by a Guatemalan man named Hector, they served some of the best Souvlaki Henderson had ever tasted.

When they were seated, Wilson removed a thin laptop from its leather case and powered it on.

Henderson glanced over at the screen. The background was wallpapered with an illustration of John Travolta and Samuel L. Jackson from *Pulp Fiction*. Travolta's head, though, had been replaced with Darth Vader's, and Jackson's by Boba Fet.

*What the hell is wrong with this kid?* Henderson thought.

He turned his attention away from the screen as the server approached, a tiny woman, maybe four and a half feet tall, who wore oversized red glasses that gave her an owlish look.

"Hola, gentlemen," she said. "Can I get you started with something to drink?"

"Just water for me," Henderson said.

"I'll have a Coke," Wilson answered. "And can I get the password for your Wi-Fi network?"

"Of course," she replied. "It's pitaparty123."

Wilson quickly typed the password into the network settings and watched as the Wi-Fi icon lit up. "Perfect. Thank you." He cracked his knuckles. "Alright. Let me show you how this baby works."

He removed the USB drive from his pocket and inserted it into a port on the side of the computer. A few seconds later, a small picture of a hard drive popped onto the screen above Darth Vader's head.

Wilson double-clicked the image of the drive and, as it opened, the *Pulp Fiction* wallpaper was replaced by an animated picture of a blonde woman in a bikini holding a surfboard. A speech bubble popped up by her mouth: "U dun been hacked," before popping like a balloon and repeating the process a second later.

"Pretty sweet, huh?" Wilson asked.

Henderson didn't look amused. "I guess. But what does it do?"

Wilson quickly removed a second laptop from the leather case and placed it on the table next to the first. "Now we fire up this computer and connect it to the hot spot on my phone."

He punched a few keys on the second computer and, satisfied with the results, moused over an icon of a skull and crossbones, and double clicked.

The screen lit up with what looked like a makeshift

analytics dashboard. "I haven't had time to pretty this up, but the application works flawlessly."

He clicked a couple more buttons, and the dashboard was replaced by a different screen—the restaurant's Quick-Books account. "I see the Gyros are selling well this month."

Wilson pointed to a line item on the page and turned the screen to show Henderson. "Now we have access to everything that's on this network—computers, cell phones, servers—everything. We have complete visibility into all the programs, emails, search history and anything else we want to see."

"Not bad," Henderson said, suddenly impressed with the kid. "Not bad at all."

"And this computer?" Wilson pointed to the first one with the blonde on the screen. "This computer is locked now. No way to access it unless I push the magic button." He pressed a red stop sign-shaped icon on the second computer and the blonde disappeared, returning the screen to *Pulp Fiction*. "I can lock down every device connected to this network and, unless you're one of the world's top hackers, you're not going to unlock it."

Henderson had to admit, the kid had done a bang-up job. *This might actually work.* One little USB drive had a chance to bring down the most powerful cartel in all of Mexico. He put a hand on Wilson's shoulder and squeezed. "Looks like I'm buying lunch tomorrow, too."

---

After dropping off Reynolds at the Consulate building, Anna and Danny began the thirty-minute drive to the Gran Terraza. The massive shopping mall sat in the Colonia Oblatos area of the city and housed over seventy stores and restaurants, with a large food court that dominated the second floor.

Anna had taken Danny to this mall when he was a small boy and thought it would be the perfect place to meet Juan—very public, with lots of cameras and lots of security.

Weekends were a busy time at the shopping center, and the parking lot was nearly full. After a couple of laps around the building, Anna found an empty spot toward the rear and nosed the Corolla in between two large SUVs.

Danny marveled at the massive building. It was modern and clean, with slate-covered walls on the ground floor that transitioned up into glossy orange panels streaked with shards of white, then transitioned further into a charcoal gray cap that formed the roofline.

Logos hung from the gray cap advertising the movie theaters, clothing stores and restaurants awaiting within the building.

"This place is huge." Danny said, a bit intimidated by the structure.

"I brought you here years ago. I pushed you around the stores in your stroller and bought you an ice cream from the Dairy Queen. You thought it was the best treat you'd ever had."

"I don't remember," Danny said.

"You were very young." Anna removed the phone from her purse and stopped on the sidewalk in front of the entrance.

"Are you texting him?" Danny asked.

"Yes, I'm going to tell him we'll meet at the food court. We can talk there."

She thumbed at the screen for a moment and returned the phone to her purse. "Ready?"

Danny nodded, and they started through the automatic doors.

Inside the mall, the air was cool and smelled of delicious food. There were people everywhere, buzzing from store-to-store toting bags of clothing, shoes and other merchandise.

They stepped onto a large stainless steel and glass escalator connecting the first floor with the second and coasted upwards, until they reached the food court.

Much like the rest of the building, the food court was modern and colorful. The space was covered by a massive aluminum pergola covered in strands of LED lights and supported by large columns covered in decorative wooden slats.

There were restaurants everywhere—American places like Subway, Carl's Jr. and Starbucks were interspersed with local places like Tozca and iL TaVolo.

Anna chose a table halfway between two of the giant columns, each of which had a security camera mounted to the front and back. They would be safe here—within clear view of the cameras and among dozens of other tables filled with hungry shoppers.

"Are we going to get something to eat?" Danny asked, perpetually hungry.

"It's almost two o'clock. Let's wait for Juan to get here, then we can order something."

She scanned the courtyard. It was filled with people, but none of them were Juan. His appearance had probably changed over the years, but she was confident she would still be able to recognize him.

Anna shifted her gaze to the escalators. There was a young family, a father with a mother holding a baby in a carrier strapped to her chest. Behind them was a group of teenagers. Four or five kids that looked to be a couple of years older than Danny.

She stopped and paused, looking at a disheveled man behind the group of teenagers. He wore a black t-shirt over blue jeans. She scanned his face. It was covered with the beginnings of a scraggly beard, and the side of his neck was blotted with a terrible rose tattoo. How could she forget that terrible tattoo?

Anna remembered the night he'd come home with it. He'd gotten drunk at the bar, as usual, but that night a friend had bet him a few pesos he wouldn't get the tattoo. Never one to back away from a drunken challenge—or an awful choice—Juan marched into an all-night tattoo parlor near the bar and had the rose permanently inked onto his neck.

She'd laughed when she saw it. Not just at the placement on his neck, but also at the monumentally bad artwork. The lines were crooked and blown out in places. The color was blotchy and thin around the center. She often thought it looked more like an raw hunk of meat rather than a beautiful flower.

He didn't like it when she laughed at him. He had grabbed her face with his hand and clamped her cheeks together to make her stop. When the tears began to flow, Juan had released his grip and began cursing her for being such a terrible wife.

Now she watched as he rode the elevator up. She wouldn't be intimidated today.

As he stepped off the elevator and into the courtyard, Anna stood from the table.

She remembered the first time they met. It was a street festival in Villa Unión. A mariachi band played on a small stage in the park while extravagantly dressed women danced around them in unison, their dresses twirling in brightly colored waves as they moved.

Anna had been in the crowd with a group of friends, just fourteen at the time, and Juan had struck up a conversation with her. They began dating, and for the first couple of years, their connection was strong. So strong they'd gotten married when she was just sixteen and he eighteen.

But after Danny was born, the relationship took a turn for the worse. He complained that Anna was always nagging about something to do with the baby. She never wanted to go out or party with friends anymore, and he resented her for it.

He began spending more and more nights at the bar, until the night he'd gotten blackout drunk and beat her.

Juan had woken up the next morning trying to apologize. Telling her he'd never touch her again, but within days, she was gone. Wouldn't answer his calls. Wouldn't reply to his texts. Just gone.

The memories flooded back now that she saw his face.

For a moment, she considered gathering Danny and leaving, but a pang of nagging guilt made her stay.

Juan opened his arms wide as he approached the table where Danny was seated. The boy stood and reluctantly returned the hug, breathing in the stale odor of Juan's dirty shirt.

"Daniel, my son, I can't believe how big you are."

Danny stood a full two inches taller than Juan and outweighed him by twenty pounds.

Juan turned his attention to Anna, moving toward her and opening his arms again.

Anna took a step back and extended a hand. "Hola, Juan," she said flatly.

Juan stopped and took her hand. "Thank you for meeting me, Anna. You really made my day."

"Should we order something to eat?" Anna asked, studying Juan's face. The man looked like hell, but he looked more hungover than sick. He didn't sound ill either, like he had on the phone earlier in the day. She chalked it up to paranoia.

Juan looked at Danny. "You hungry, Daniel?"

Anna huffed. If the guy had seen his son once or twice in the past fourteen years, he'd know Danny was *always* hungry.

"Yeah," Danny replied. "Do you like Subway?"

"Sure, son. Whatever you want."

They ordered two turkey and cheese sandwiches, one for Anna and one for Danny. Juan settled on a footlong meatball sub.

After taking their orders, a teenage boy behind the counter said, "That'll be four hundred and twenty pesos."

Juan looked at Anna sheepishly. "I'm afraid I'm a bit short."

She shook her head and removed a few bills from her purse. *Same old Juan.*

As they ate, Juan asked Danny about school and friends and girls—pretending to care about important events in the boy's life.

Danny's answers were always short and guarded.

His father was not at all what he'd imagined. Danny wasn't sure how he imagined the man would look, but he knew this wasn't it. *This* man was dirty and unkempt and had terrible table manners, wiping his lips with his hand instead of a napkin and talking with his mouth full of food. Those types of behaviors wouldn't fly in his mother's home.

*Maybe that's why she left him.*

Anna watched intently as the two talked. She studied Juan in particular. Aside from being a disgustingly sloppy eater, he had wolfed down the footlong sandwich in just a couple of minutes. In her experience, sick people didn't have much of an appetite. Again, she chalked it up to paranoia, but made a mental note.

They continued their conversation until nearly two

thirty, with Juan doing most of the talking and Danny adding a polite yes or no in between bites of his sandwich.

The reunion wasn't going the way Danny had anticipated and Anna sensed his unease. She began gathering the sandwich wrappers, placing them on the plastic tray in front of her, and stood from the table. "I'm afraid that's all the time we have, Juan."

Without protest, he jumped up from his chair. "Thank you again for meeting me," he said. "Daniel, I'm sorry we didn't do this sooner."

He gave Danny another hug and looked at Anna. "Can I walk you to your car?"

She guessed he wanted to squeeze in a bit more time with Danny, then sighed. "Alright."

He smiled and pointed toward the escalator. "After you."

As they rode down the escalator, Juan removed a phone from his pocket and began furiously moving his thumbs across the screen, texting. When Anna looked at him, he tilted the phone so she couldn't see. *Probably talking to some bimbo from the bar*, she thought.

They rode down the escalator and headed through the large automatic doors at the front of the mall. The sudden burst of sunlight outside made them squint as they exited the building and began winding through the parking lot.

As they approached the small Corolla, Anna noticed the SUVs bracketing her car were gone. Now a large black Cadillac Escalade was parked in front of her.

As she approached the car, two men, one tall and one short, exited the Escalade and headed directly for them. She grabbed Danny's arm instinctively, her sense of danger piqued at the sight of the men walking towards them.

The taller man looked around and removed a pistol from his waistband, moving close to Danny and pointing it at his side. "You scream, the boy dies."

The shorter man grabbed Anna by the arm. "Get in the car."

Anna looked at Juan and mouthed, "Help us."

He shook his head and gave a villainous smile. "Afraid I can't do that, Anna. These men need to talk to you."

*Dammit!* She gritted her teeth. How could she have been so stupid? The bastard had sold them out.

As the short man led Anna and Danny to the SUV, Juan called to him. "Hey, what about my money?"

The shorter man stared back at Juan for a moment, then looked at the taller man. "Give him his reward."

The tall man nodded, approached Juan slowly and reached into his pocket. But instead of the roll of hundreds, the tall man brandished a heavy set of brass knuckles. Without warning, he threw a vicious straight right into Juan's face, smashing his nose. Blood gushed and Juan fell to the ground, pawing at his battered face. He moaned and seemed to drift in and out of consciousness as he lay there, blood pooling on the asphalt.

The tall man looked down at him as he struggled, studying him like an ant he'd just burned under a magnifying glass. He removed a twenty-peso coin from his pocket and flipped it into the air, watching as it landed on the pavement and bounced near Juan's face. "Don't spend it all in one place, cabron."

# CHAPTER 17

Agent Henderson's desk phone beeped, and a female voice with a thick New York accent droned out of the speaker, "Agent Henderson, there's a Dillon Reynolds here to see you. He says he has an appointment."

"I'll come down and get him. Tell him to wait out front."

The line clicked, and Henderson rose from his desk, heading to the lobby to collect Reynolds.

As he approached the front doors, Henderson punched a code into a stainless-steel keypad mounted to the wall. The door buzzed, then clicked. He pushed it open, allowing Reynolds to come inside.

"How's it going, Dillon?" Henderson asked, extending a hand. "Where are Anna and Danny?"

Reynolds returned the handshake. "They had ..." He paused. "... another meeting, so it's just me today."

Henderson sensed Reynolds' hesitation, but didn't press him further.

Once they were seated in his office, Henderson said. "I'm going to bring in another agent to help me explain our idea." He picked up the phone and pushed a button, causing it to glow red.

"Wilson," answered the voice on the other end.

"Wilson, it's Henderson. Dillon Reynolds is here. I'd like you to come explain the idea behind your virus."

"Sure thing. Be there in two minutes."

*Virus?* Reynolds wondered silently.

As they waited, Henderson asked, "Any luck getting ID for Anna and Danny?"

"Some," Reynolds said. "We got Anna's driver's license, but we still need to get Danny's birth certificate, which we can't do until the Civil Registry opens tomorrow."

Both men looked up as Benjamin Wilson appeared at the office door. "Mr. Reynolds, I'm Agent Ben Wilson."

Reynolds stood and shook the man's hand, then all three seated themselves.

"Start from the beginning," Henderson said, pointing at Wilson.

Much as he'd done that afternoon, Wilson launched into a high-level explanation of what the virus was, what it could do and how they could use it to hurt the cartel.

Reynolds listened intently. He didn't understand all the technical mumbo jumbo, but he got the general idea behind the virus.

When Wilson had wrapped up the explanation, Henderson looked at Reynolds. "There's just one problem."

Reynolds raised his eyebrows. "What?"

"We've got to figure out a way to get the drive into Aguado's hands without him becoming suspicious."

Reynolds waited for Henderson to propose a solution, but none came. Then, after a few awkward seconds, the reality dawned on him. "Are you saying you want *me* to get the drive back to Aguado?"

Both agents nodded apprehensively.

"I'm not sure if you misunderstood my story yesterday,

but we're trying to get as far *away* from Aguado as possible, not the other way around."

"I understand your concern, Dillon, but this could be a way to solve your problem with the cartel once and for all."

"What about the visas?" Reynolds asked.

"Sure, I can get you the visas. And you can go back to the States and maybe Anna and Danny can stay. Or maybe they can't. Hopefully, you understand we don't have any control when it comes to immigration issues."

"That's a risk I'm willing to take," Reynolds said.

Henderson continued the full court press. "Okay. Then what? Do you really want to live the rest of your life looking over your shoulder? Do you want Anna and Danny to have to do the same? The cartel doesn't recognize borders, you know."

Reynolds had just assumed that, once they were back home, they'd be safe. But now it occurred to him that the cartel could probably get to them just as easily in the U.S. as they could in Mexico. Why hadn't he thought of that before?

Henderson was right, they'd be sitting ducks, and he didn't want to live the rest of his life looking over his shoulder. He considered the idea for a moment. Maybe it *was* time to go on the offensive.

Henderson could sense Reynolds weighing his options and went for the close. "Look Dillon, I'm going to level with you. This is a risky proposition, and I can't guarantee the outcome. But I'll have a team of our best agents follow you wherever they take you. Once Aguado checks the drive to make sure it's real, his systems will all be under our control. Then we'll execute the takedown. He'll be in cuffs before he knows what's happening."

Reynolds exhaled deeply. "So how do I get to Aguado? It's not like I have his home address."

"You mentioned the crooked cop when we talked yesterday. You thought he was wrapped up in this somehow. What made you think that?"

"After he pulled us over, he didn't say why he stopped us, just asked Anna for her driver's license. Then I watched him in the rear-view mirror when he went back to his car. He didn't call in the stop with his radio. He used a cell phone to call someone instead. It just felt wrong."

"How did you manage to get away from him?" Henderson asked.

Reynolds swallowed hard. During their first conversation he'd been purposely vague about the encounter on the side of the highway, but now he knew the time for half-truths was over. "I wasn't totally honest with you yesterday. The cop was roughing me up and threatening to do worse to Anna. I thought he was going to follow through, so I ..." He paused, trying to find the words. "... I beat the shit out of him."

Henderson and Wilson shot a sideways glance at each other.

"You beat the shit out of him?" Henderson prodded.

"Yeah, I knocked him out cold and dragged his body down an embankment away from the road. When I got into his car to roll it down the ravine, I looked at his phone and the last call was to Miguel Alvarez."

"How do you think the cop knew which car to pull over?"

"He must have gotten the license plate number somehow. That's the only thing I can think of."

Henderson tensed, and his eyes widened slightly. "So, Anna's out there driving around with those plates on the car still?"

"No, no. We pulled over at a gas station and I borrowed a plate from another car in the parking lot. That's how we made it the rest of the way here with no trouble."

"You *borrowed* a plate?" Henderson chided.

"I mean, if you want to get technical, I guess you could say I stole it."

Henderson paused, gathering his thoughts, then cleared his throat. "So, what I heard you say was, you got pulled over, then sped away from a man you thought was impersonating a police officer. You have no idea who assaulted him, or who drove his car into a ditch. Am I understanding you correctly?"

"Ye ... Yeah, that's what happened." Reynolds stumbled over his words.

"Good," Henderson replied. "Now that we're all on the same page, we need to figure out how to get you and the drive to Aguado."

He looked across the desk at both Reynolds and Wilson. "I'm open to suggestions."

Reynolds looked at the floor, staring blankly, searching for an idea when it hit him. "Ed Hernandez!" he said, looking up wide-eyed at Henderson.

"Who's Ed Hernandez?" Wilson asked.

"He runs the Baseball Academy where I coach." Reynolds could see the confusion among the two agents and explained. "Saturday morning, after the incident at dinner the previous night, I was going to go ask Ed for advice on how to deal with the drive. We started talking, but someone interrupted us. Ed had to go downstairs, but he left his phone on the desk. When it buzzed, I looked at the screen and it read Miguel Alvarez. I recognized the name from the letter."

Henderson narrowed his eyes. "So, you think this Ed Hernandez is involved with the cartel somehow?"

"I think he is. Plus, after I saw Alvarez's name on Ed's phone, I grabbed Danny, and we left the Academy. Hernandez panicked when he couldn't find us. He must have called and texted twenty times, asking us to come back."

"Do you think he just might have been concerned that you took one of the players from the Academy and didn't say where you were going?" Wilson asked.

"Possibly," Reynolds replied. "But why would Alvarez call him first thing in the morning the day after we got the drive? The timing is too perfect."

Henderson didn't disagree. If this Ed Hernandez had a direct line to Alvarez, he could certainly get to Aguado, too. "Okay, I think we've got our way in. It'll take me some time to put together a team of agents, but I should be able to get something together in the next few days. We'll also need to alert the FBI. If Hernandez takes you somewhere, the FBI will be able to assist in the raid, since we can frame it as kidnapping at that point."

"What about the Mexican authorities?" Reynolds asked.

"I've got that covered, too," Henderson replied. "A good friend of mine is a Chief Inspector in the Mexican Federal Police—he owes me a favor. I'll clear everything through his department."

"What should I do in the meantime?" Reynolds asked.

"Lay low. All of you. Where did you say you were staying?"

"Some flea bag hotel in Tepic."

"Perfect," Henderson replied. "Stay in your room as much as possible and park Anna's car somewhere off the street so it's not visible. I'll call you when we're ready to contact Hernandez."

―――

After the meeting with Henderson, Reynolds leaned against

the concrete planter box in front of the Consulate texting Anna.

> "Hey, call me when you can."

He clicked send and waited for a reply. Five minutes, ten minutes, then fifteen minutes went by—no reply.

Reynolds didn't like it. Was she in trouble? Had the meetup with Juan gone sideways? He took a deep breath and tried to push the thoughts out of his head. She had probably just missed the text. He removed the phone from his pocket again and sent another message.

> "Anna, did you see my last text? Call me back. Thanks."

Another five minutes passed without a reply. Now his mind was racing with all manner of sinister scenarios.

Reynolds checked the phone for the umpteenth time in the last few minutes—nothing. He thumbed over the screen and pulled up Anna's contact information, then pressed the call button and waited for a ring.

As he put the phone to his ear, Reynolds heard the high-pitched whine of a small engine buzzing toward him. He looked up to see two teenagers on an old scooter, barreling down the sidewalk.

The driver swerved towards Reynolds while the passenger extended an arm and yanked the phone from Reynolds' hand.

"Hey!" he screamed after the thieves, looking around wildly. "Those guys stole my phone!"

No one on the sidewalk stopped. Their heads turned at the commotion, but they kept about their business.

Reynolds began sprinting after the scooter as it bounced over the curb and veered back into the street. The driver throttled up the engine and a puff of black smoke coughed from the exhaust as the scooter accelerated south.

His lungs burned and his legs ached as Reynolds gave chase, racing down the street, trying to close the distance between him and the scooter. But as the chase wore on, the thieves gained ground. Each passing second put more distance between them and their pursuer, the whine of the small engine growing fainter before finally fading into the noise of the city.

"Shit!" Reynolds sucked in huge gasps of air. This was the last thing he needed. Now he had no way of contacting Anna. He didn't even know her phone number, since it was programmed into the phone.

He put a hand in his back pocket, feeling for the envelope—it was still there.

As he walked back to the Consulate, a thousand thoughts swirled through his head. Not only couldn't he call Anna, now he no longer had Ed's cell number either.

Reynolds muttered under his breath as he walked, cursing himself as much as the thieves.

*Should have seen them coming.*

Back in front of the Consulate, Reynolds approached the service window and asked the woman with the New York accent to see Agent Henderson, who appeared shortly after at the front door.

"Forget something?" the agent asked.

"Yeah, I forgot to check my surroundings."

The agent looked puzzled.

"Two kids just stole my phone and took off with it on a scooter," Reynolds explained.

Henderson sighed. "Unfortunately, that's a common occurrence around here."

"Yeah, well, now I don't have any way to contact Anna. Ed Hernandez's cell phone number was in there too."

The agent motioned for Reynolds to come through the door. "C'mon in. Let me see if I can help you out."

Reynolds entered the building, and both men headed back to Henderson's office. The agent seated himself behind his desk and began typing away at the keyboard in front of him. "I think I should be able to dig up Anna's cell number pretty easily." He paused and clicked a few more buttons. "Here it is." He scribbled the number on a scrap of paper and slid it across the desk to Reynolds. "You can use my office line if you like."

"Thanks." Reynolds picked up the receiver. He quickly punched in the phone number and waited. The phone rang seven times, then went to voicemail: *"Hola, this is Anna. Please leave a message after the beep."*

Reynolds hung up the phone. "No answer." He gave Henderson a grim stare. "She didn't answer my texts earlier, either."

"You said she was at a meeting?" Henderson asked.

"Sort of," Reynolds replied. "Her ex-husband called and said he was sick, some kind of terminal illness, and he wanted to see Danny one last time."

The agent raised an eyebrow. "And you believed that?"

"Not for a second, but she insisted on giving Danny the choice to see him or not, and Danny chose to see him."

Henderson mulled over the information. "I don't like it. The timing is too coincidental."

Reynolds nodded.

"Where was this meeting supposed to take place?" the agent asked.

"At a mall. I think it's called the Gran Terraza. We both thought it would be a safe place for them to meet, since they have cameras and security everywhere."

Henderson rose from his desk and looked at Reynolds. The last thing he wanted was for Reynolds to be focused on the missing woman instead of getting the drive to Aguado, which meant they had to find her quickly. "Looks like we're headed to the mall." He said, and scooped a set of keys off the desk.

The ride to the mall was nearly thirty minutes—some of the longest of Reynolds' life. As they drove, his mind drifted from one sinister scenario to the next, none of them playing out in Anna and Danny's favor.

He should have gone with her, should've just postponed the meeting with Henderson and convinced her to let him accompany them to the mall. How could he have been so stupid?

As they approached the mall, Henderson's voice roused Reynolds from his thoughts. "What kind of car does Anna drive? I want to search the parking lot before we head inside."

"It's a tan-colored Corolla, older and pretty beat up."

"You take the left side and I'll take the right," Henderson said as they wound the car up and down each aisle, searching for the car.

"There it is," Reynolds shouted, pointing a finger. "Over there, in the back."

Henderson spotted the little compact and steered the sedan to where it was parked.

Both men got out of the car, scanning the surrounding area. There were no people and no other vehicles parked near Anna's car.

Henderson checked the driver's side door. "It's locked."

Reynolds checked the passenger side—also locked.

"Think she's still in the mall?" Henderson asked.

"Let's hope so."

As they started towards the building, Henderson put an arm in front of Reynolds. "Stop!"

Reynolds looked startled. "What?"

Henderson squatted down and pointed. "Look here, at the asphalt. That's fresh blood."

Reynolds squatted beside him and looked at the ground. A dark circle created by a sticky pool of blood lay just fifteen feet from Anna's car.

"Shit," Reynolds said, almost at a whisper. "This isn't good."

Henderson shook his head. "No, it's not. We need to check inside, quickly."

They jogged to the front of the building and into the cool air of the shopping center.

"It'll be faster if we split up," Henderson instructed. "You take the second level and I'll take the first. Meet me back here in fifteen minutes."

Reynolds nodded and made a beeline for the escalator. At the top, he quickly scanned the food court, wending his way through the tables and chairs. Next, he moved to the row of shops to the right of the food court, checking each one before returning to the stores on the left side of the food court.

There was no sign of Anna or Danny anywhere.

He returned to the escalator and descended to the ground floor where Henderson was waiting. "Anything?"

The agent shook his head. "Nothing."

"On our way into the building, I noticed security cameras mounted to the light posts in the parking lot. We've got to check the footage."

"Agreed, but I have no jurisdiction here. I can't just barge into the security office and demand to see the surveillance video."

"I bet the security guys here don't know that," Reynolds replied.

"You're going to get me fired," Henderson muttered. "But

if we're going to do this, you need to look the part, too. Stay here. I'll be back in a few minutes."

As promised, Henderson returned minutes later toting a black tactical vest that had a large *DEA* embroidered on a patch affixed to the front with Velcro.

"Put this on."

Reynolds donned the vest, and the two headed for a small kiosk illustrating a directory of stores and their location.

"Right here." Reynolds pointed at a tiny blue square that contained a white security badge. "Down this hallway next to the bathrooms."

They hurried down a brightly lit corridor that led to the Security Office. Inside, a man dressed in a wrinkled blue uniform and a baseball cap reading SECURITY sat with his feet propped on an L-shaped desk, watching a bank of television monitors.

He quickly removed his feet from the desk and stood when Henderson and Reynolds walked into the office. "This is a restricted area," he said. "The bathrooms are down the hall."

Henderson quickly flipped out a credential case and presented it for the security guard to examine. "I'm agent Henderson with the United States Drug Enforcement Agency. This is my partner, Agent Reynolds. We need to see the surveillance footage from the east parking lot from this afternoon."

The man studied the ID, not really sure what he should be looking for. "I'll have to call my supervisor."

"We don't have time for that. We have reason to believe a violent crime has recently been committed on this property and the longer we wait, the less chance we have to catch the suspect."

*This acting thing wasn't that hard after all,* Henderson thought.

"I'm guessing something like that happening right under your nose wouldn't look good to your supervisor."

The man thought about this for a minute. It had been quiet all day, nothing unusual. Then again, he'd taken a quick nap after lunch. Maybe that's when the crime had occurred.

Henderson continued, "I don't have to mention that in my report, though. I can say the incident took place off the property, but I need you to cooperate—now."

The security guard shrugged. "Okay, but make it quick. Shift change is in thirty minutes."

"We'll be in and out of here before you know it," Henderson said. "Now scroll back to around one forty-five this afternoon. We need to see the camera facing the back of the east lot."

The guard did as he was instructed, pulling up a clear shot of the east parking lot.

As the video began playing, Henderson said, "Speed it up, please."

The guard hit a button on the computer keyboard and the video began playing faster. Cars jockeyed in and out of the lot while people walked quickly back and forth down the aisles.

"Slow it down," Reynolds instructed.

The guard slowed the video to normal speed. Anna had just pulled the Corolla into the parking lot. They watched as she and Danny exited the vehicle and proceeded into the mall.

"Nothing there," Henderson said. "Speed it up again."

They waited five agonizingly long minutes, watching the timestamp on the video quickly tick through the minutes of the afternoon. Finally, Anna and Danny emerged from the mall. They were accompanied by a man.

"That's got to be Juan," Reynolds said.

"Slow it down again," Henderson instructed.

The video slowed, clearly showing Anna, Danny, and Juan approach her car. As they did, two men exited a large, black Cadillac Escalade.

"Can you zoom in here?" Henderson asked.

The guard clicked his mouse, and the video zoomed in, making the footage much grainier.

One of the men neared Danny. Henderson squinted into the footage, struggling to make out what looked like a gun in the man's hand. He pointed it in Danny's side and said something to Anna.

As the video progressed, they watched the scene play out as Alvarez led Anna and Danny to the SUV and Zapata knocked Juan senseless with the vicious right hand.

"Can you zoom in on the license plate on the SUV?" Henderson asked.

The guard complied and Henderson snatched a pen from the desk and quickly jotted the plate number on a sticky note.

"Thanks for your cooperation," Henderson said. "I'll make a note of your assistance in my report."

The guard straightened a little in his seat, suddenly proud to have been such a valuable part of the investigation.

Reynolds removed the DEA vest as they walked back to the car. "How quick can you get a fix on that plate number?"

"Seconds. The technology now-a-days makes things much more efficient."

Henderson pulled a cell phone from his pocket and dialed. "Wilson, I need you to get some info on a plate number." He continued reading the number and waited as Wilson fed it into the computer system.

There was a brief pause, after which Henderson replied, "Got it," and ended the call.

He stopped walking and looked at Reynolds. "The Escalade is registered to a corporation—Eldorado Finance."

A shock of panic swept through Reynolds' body as he heard the name. "That's the name that was on the loan documents at the Academy." He could barely utter the words.

"Dillon." Henderson's face hardened, and his voice became robotic. "I think we have to assume the Cartel has Anna and Danny."

## CHAPTER 18

"Give me your purse," Alvarez demanded.

Anna handed him the bag and peeked through the windshield, watching as Juan writhed on the ground, bleeding all over the asphalt. Despite her current situation, she felt a twinge of vindication seeing the deadbeat in so much agony.

"Where is it?" Alvarez growled, rummaging through Anna's purse.

"Where is what?" Anna replied.

Alvarez slammed an open palm directly into Anna's face. She recoiled in pain and surprise, and Danny instinctively reached for Alvarez's hand, grabbing it to prevent him from striking another blow.

As he struggled with Alvarez, Danny felt something hard press against the side of his forehead.

Zapata had returned to the car and was turned around in the driver's seat, holding the barrel of his pistol against Danny's temple. "Do that again and I'll splatter your brains all over your mother."

Danny slowly released his grip on the much smaller

Alvarez and scowled at Zapata as they pulled out of the parking lot.

Zapata steered the SUV through the streets surrounding the mall, winding further into the city before pulling the Escalade into a narrow alley lined with cars and trucks on one side. He eased the vehicle to a stop behind a white Ford pickup truck with AC/DC stickers plastered all over the rear window.

Alvarez looked at Anna. "This is the last time I will ask politely. Where is it?"

Her face still burning from the slap, Anna decided not to play coy. "I don't know. Dillon has it and I don't know where he is."

"Get out," Alvarez demanded. "Walk to the back of the vehicle."

Danny and Anna took turns stepping out of the Escalade and walked to the rear of the bulky SUV. They were both immediately slammed against the lift gate and frisked. Anna's skin crawled as Alvarez ran his hands up and down her body, checking for the drive.

"Anything?" he asked Zapata.

"Nope, the kid's clean," Zapata answered.

Satisfied with his pat down of Anna, Alvarez barked, "Turn around."

They watched as Alvarez dumped the contents of Anna's purse on the ground and knelt to sort through the pile of coins, lip balm, sticks of gum and other oddities. There was no USB drive.

As he sifted through the contents of the purse, Alvarez plucked a crisp white business card from the pile. He flipped it over and read:

**United States Department of Justice**
**Drug Enforcement Administration**

Frank Henderson
Senior Special Agent
Guadalajara, Mexico Field Office
C. Progreso 175, Col Americana, Americana, 44100
Guadalajara, Jal., Mexico
Office: +52 33 8526 5555
Cell: +52 24 9671 5555
frank.henderson@usdoj.gov

"What the hell is this?" Alvarez held the card in front of Anna's face. "What are you doing talking to the DEA?"

Her heart sank as she remembered slipping the card in her purse after the initial meeting with Henderson. There was no way to explain the card, so she opted to be somewhat truthful in her explanation.

"We met with Agent Henderson yesterday. He was going to help us get expedited visas so we could go to the U.S. We didn't tell them about the drive. I promise."

Alvarez growled and removed a phone from his pocket. "Jefe, we've got the woman and the kid."

A pause.

"No, she didn't have it on her. But there's something else. She had a business card from the DEA in her purse."

Another pause as Alvarez listened.

"Of course, Jefe."

He replaced the phone in his pocket and turned back to Anna. "Where is the gringo?"

Anna's mind raced, frantically searching for a way to lead them away from Reynolds. "I told you—I don't know. We split up this morning. He said he had some errands to run while we were at the mall."

Alvarez studied her face for a few long seconds. Presumably, she thought, to determine if she was telling the truth.

"Call him," Alvarez said, retrieving Anna's phone from

the pile on the ground. He handed the phone to her and continued, "Tell him to meet us to meet us here with the drive in thirty minutes. For every minute he's late, we'll take one of the boy's fingers."

Anna recoiled at the thought of Alvarez torturing her son. "But what if he's more than thirty minutes away?"

"Then your son will never throw a baseball again." Alvarez said flatly. "And tell him to come alone. If we see any sign of the DEA, the boy dies."

Anna gritted her teeth. The thought of these scumbags hurting Danny filled her with rage, making her hands shake as she held the phone and clicked on Reynolds' number. She listened as the line rang and rang. No answer, no voicemail, just kept ringing. "He's not picking up."

Alvarez exhaled and rolled his neck from side to side, releasing a series of cracks and pops. "Call him again."

Again, Anna dialed the number. Again, the line rang and rang.

"Text him," Alvarez demanded.

Anna clicked the text icon and began typing out a message. Alvarez moved closer as she typed, watching the screen. She could feel his breath on her neck and a wave of nausea swept over her. She coughed to put some space between their faces, drew in a deep breath to settle herself, then held up the phone for Alvarez to examine.

He nodded in approval. "Send it."

They waited an excruciatingly long ten minutes for a response. Anna racked her brain for a solution or an escape plan, but none came. Every scenario ended in Danny getting hurt or worse, and that wasn't a risk she was willing to take.

She looked down at the phone. The screen remained blank. "Why wasn't Dillon answering? He always had his phone on him. Was he in trouble? The cartel clearly didn't have him, so where could he be?"

"Anything?" Alvarez growled.

Anna slowly shook her head, terrified at what might happen next.

Alvarez removed the phone from his pocket and dialed Aguado. "He's not answering, Jefe."

There was a long pause as Aguado gave instructions.

"Alright, we'll head your way in twenty minutes."

Alvarez turned his attention back to Anna. "Give me your phone and get back in the car."

Anna was relieved when Alvarez took the passenger seat instead of sitting in the back beside her again.

Alvarez looked at Zapata. "He said to wait another twenty minutes, then head back."

The driver nodded and continued scanning the alleyway, looking in his rear-view mirror every few seconds to monitor both entrances.

The twenty minutes came and went. Reynolds neither returned the call nor texted. Anna knew there was a problem. Dillon would never abandon them like this. She began to fear he was hurt—or dead. She shuddered and forced her mind to think positively. *Maybe he lost his phone, or the battery died. Yes, that's probably what happened.* At least, that was the explanation she wanted to believe right now.

"The coward isn't going to show," Alvarez finally said to Zapata. "Let's get out of here."

Zapata put the car in drive and the Escalade pulled out of the alley and headed for the highway.

"Where are you taking us?" Anna asked.

"Put your seat belt on and shut up," Alvarez replied. "It's going to be a long ride."

Reynolds flexed and released the muscles in his forearms, just as he'd done before he beat up the crooked cop. The cartel had taken two people he cared for, and he could feel the rage welling up inside him.

"You, okay?" Henderson asked, feeling Reynolds' tension.

"No, I'm not okay. When I get my hands on these pieces of shit, they'll wish they'd never heard of Anna and Danny."

"Easy, Dillon. We need to take this one step at a time and go through the proper channels."

"No way, I'm done messing around," Reynolds spat back. "I'm going to call Ed when we get back to the Consulate. If they want the drive, they can have it. It's right here in my pocket."

"Dillon, we don't even have a team in place yet. You'll be walking into the meeting blind with no backup."

"I don't care. What do you think they'll do when they find out Anna and Danny don't have the drive? You know as well as I do, they'll use try to use them as leverage to get the drive back. The only problem is, they have no way of contacting me. I don't even have a damn cell phone anymore!" He slammed his fist on the dash, shaking the interior of the sedan.

Henderson exhaled a deep breath, but didn't reply. He knew Reynolds was furious and didn't want to push him any further, hoping he would calm down by the time they reached the Consulate.

They rode the rest of the way in silence. When they finally reached the Consulate, Henderson waited as the gate guarding the employee parking lot slowly slid open.

As they exited the vehicle, he said, "What did you mean when you said you have the drive in your pocket? I thought it was at your bank in Mazatlán?"

Reynolds pulled the envelope from his back pocket and

held it up. "If there's one thing I've learned over the last few days, it's not to trust anyone."

"Do you trust me, Dillon?" Henderson asked.

"You've proven yourself to be an ally so far," Reynolds replied guardedly.

"Then let me help you. Don't go off and do this Rambo shit. Let me put a team together so we can do this the right way."

Reynolds stared back but didn't respond.

"I'm not saying we can't make something happen quickly. I'm just asking you to give me a little time. Can you do that?"

"Okay." Reynolds sighed. "But I'm trusting you Henderson. Don't burn me on this."

"You have my word," Henderson replied.

As they approached the building, the agent removed a plastic ID badge from his pocket and held it against a gray box adjacent to an entry door. The box beeped and the door clicked open, allowing them into the building.

"I'm going to start making some calls. It's going to be tough sledding this late in the afternoon on a Sunday, but I'll do my best."

"Fair enough," Reynolds said.

They walked down the center of a long hallway dotted with heavy wooden doors every few feet. Henderson stopped at one of them. It had a plaque glued to the door that read *Conference Room*.

He opened the door and flicked on a light switch, revealing a large conference table surrounded by a dozen high-backed leather chairs. A flat screen television hung from the wall at one end of the table while a small sink and refrigerator occupied the opposite wall.

Henderson picked up a television remote from the table and handed it to Reynolds. "You can hang out in here while

I get to work. There are sodas and waters in the fridge and the TV has American channels. Are you hungry?"

Reynolds perked up at this last question. "Yeah, I could use something to eat."

"No problem. I'll have something delivered."

With that, he turned and strode out of the conference room, leaving Reynolds to fumble with the buttons on the TV remote.

Forty-five minutes later, Agent Wilson walked into the conference room toting a large plastic bag. "Dinner is served, my friend. Word of advice, though, go easy on the hot sauce. It tastes good going down, but you'll pay for it in the morning." The young agent smiled.

Reynolds forced a smile in return. "Thanks for the advice. How's it going out there?"

"We're making progress," Wilson said. "Henderson has been on the phone with his contact from the Mexican Federal Police. His guy needs to run it up the chain of command, but he didn't seem to think we'd get much resistance. In the meantime, I've been working with the FBI to see if we can borrow a couple of their agents. I want to have as much manpower on hand as possible."

"When do you think we can put everything into action?" Reynolds asked.

"Too soon to tell. There are a lot of moving pieces to this operation, so we won't have a timeline for a while."

Reynolds nodded. "I'll let you get back to it, then. Thanks again for the food."

Wilson smiled. "You bet. It's the least Uncle Sam can do to say thanks for your help."

Reynolds quietly ate his meal and, for the next four hours, flipped through channel after channel on the flat screen, too distracted to pay attention to anything for more than thirty minutes at a time.

It was nearing ten o'clock, and he was exhausted from the day's events. Reynolds tried to close his eyes every so often, but sleep would never come. Each time he began to drift off, images flashed through his mind like strobes, each one a snapshot of Danny or Anna in some new and terrible version of peril.

"Anything good on?"

Reynolds turned to see Henderson standing in the doorway of the conference room beside what looked like a folding cot.

"Not really."

"I do the same thing," Henderson said. "A hundred and fifty channels and I can never find anything I like." He shrugged. "How are you holding up?"

"I'm fine," Reynolds replied. "I just wish I could help instead of sitting here. I feel useless."

Henderson took a seat in one of the chairs that surrounded the conference table. "I wouldn't worry about it. You'll see plenty of action tomorrow."

Reynolds straightened. "Tomorrow? What time?"

"Everyone will assemble here at eight in the morning."

"So, you've got a plan in place?"

"We've got *most of a plan* in place. There are still a few details to work out."

Reynolds nodded. Tomorrow seemed eons away, but at least now he had a timeline.

Henderson continued, "I don't want you going back to the hotel tonight. It's too risky. That's why I brought the cot. You can sleep here tonight."

Reynolds grimaced at the idea, but knew it didn't matter. He probably wouldn't get much sleep even if they put him up at the Ritz Carlton.

"Okay what about you?"

"I'm going to stay here and game plan for a couple more hours, then I'll head home to catch some sleep."

Reynolds paused, then said, "Level with me, Frank. Do you think this is really going to work?"

"It has to Dillon. Anna and Danny won't make it through this without us. Without you. That's why I wanted as much time as possible to put together a plan. To put it in your terms, I wanted to make sure we had our bases covered—and I think we do. But there are always hiccups. I want you to understand that. It's rare that an operation goes exactly to plan, so you'll need to be ready to pivot if that's what the situation dictates."

Reynolds smirked. "Pivot?"

"Yeah, like you *pivoted* on that dirty cop."

Henderson gave a tired smile and rose from the chair. "Now, if you'll excuse me, I've got some satellite photos to study."

As he walked to the door, Reynolds called out, "Hey, Henderson."

The agent turned, and Reynolds paused, searching for the right words. He decided simpler was better. "Thanks."

Henderson smiled. "You're welcome. Try to get some sleep."

# CHAPTER 19

They'd been in the car for hours. Anna couldn't quite tell how long since Alvarez had taken her phone, but it was dark now and had been for some time.

Exhausted, Danny leaned against his mother's shoulder, sleeping restlessly.

She wondered where they were going. They'd passed through Mazatlán twenty-five minutes ago and were heading north on a road that paralleled the coast.

At last, Anna felt the SUV slow. Danny began to stir, wearily opening his eyes.

"Where are we?" he asked, still groggy.

"A few miles north of Mazatlán," she whispered.

"Quiet!" Alvarez barked.

The Escalade turned off the highway onto a narrow dirt road. Thick vegetation lined both sides of the drive, creating the illusion of traveling down a dark tunnel.

Anna could see lights ahead from a building somewhere down the road. As they got closer, she could see it was a small structure set in front of a massive estate. A guard house perhaps.

Zapata pulled up to a towering wrought-iron gate

mounted between two sides of a thick stone wall surrounding the property. The gate was at least twelve feet tall, and intricately fabricated with flowery scrollwork wrapped like vines amongst the steel bars.

Zapata honked twice and two men armed with AR-15 rifles emerged from the guardhouse. "We're here to see Aguado," he said to one of the men.

The guard nodded and called to his companion, who returned to the guardhouse. Shortly after, each side of the gate began to swing open and the crunch of dirt turned to the rumble of cobblestone as the SUV lumbered into the compound.

They slowly wound down the drive, passing through endless tracts of freshly mowed lawns, perfectly manicured hedges, and outcroppings of palm trees surrounded by flower beds filled with tropical plants.

As the Escalade approached the house, it rolled to a stop beneath a towering porte-cochere that shielded guests from the sun and rain as they entered the palatial residence.

Alvarez and Zapata exited the vehicle, opening the rear doors so Anna and Danny could do the same.

Two more guards, again armed with AR-15 rifles, stood protecting a set of large wooden double doors. Alvarez nodded at one of the guards and he pushed open the heavy door, its hinges squeaking to announce their arrival.

Anna marveled at the grand entry. It was the most lavish design she had ever seen—much more luxurious and expensive than even the best resorts in Mazatlán.

The floors were made of polished stone, marbled with dark veins of black and brown running like a conflux of rivers through the entryway. On either side of the room, two elegant staircases curled upwards, meeting in the middle of a second-floor balcony lined with a gold-plated railing. Overhead, a massive chandelier hung from the ceiling, bouncing soft yellow light through thousands of tiny crystals.

"This way," Alvarez grumbled, pushing Anna down a hall and towards a set of double doors to their left.

Zapata opened one of the doors and the group entered Aguado's lavish study.

"So, this is the cause of all my problems," Aguado mused, examining Anna and Danny from his desk.

She recognized his picture from the news. The man's name was Arturo Aguado—the head of the Sinaloa Cartel. She swallowed hard, knowing they were deep in the heart of the lion's den now.

"Sit down," Alvarez ordered, pushing them towards the sofa, then seated himself next to Danny.

"We searched them both," Alvarez began. "Neither of them had the drive. She says the gringo has it, but we can't get ahold of him—he won't answer her calls or texts."

"Looks like your boyfriend is a coward, Ms. Rincon," Aguado said, staring at Anna.

"He could kick your ass!" Danny spat back.

Alvarez raised a hand to slap the boy before Aguado barked, "Wait!"

His hand slowly dropped, and Alvarez gritted his teeth.

Aguado chuckled. "Relax Miguel, looks like this one has more courage than the gringo."

Danny glared back at Aguado as he continued.

"Ms. Rincon, why is your boyfriend not answering you?"

"He's not my boyfriend," Anna snapped back. "And I don't know why he's not answering. Maybe his phone is dead."

"Convenient time to run out of battery, don't you think?"

When Anna didn't respond, Aguado continued, "I think he's a coward, and he abandoned you. That's what I think. Why would you want to protect a man like that?"

"He's not a coward, Mr. Aguado," Anna said with an icy stare.

"Ah, so you know who I am. Is that the problem? You must understand I'm not the monster they make me out to be on television. I'm a reasonable man, and I promise you the sooner we find the gringo, the sooner we get the drive back, the sooner you can all be on your way. So why don't you just tell us where he is?"

Anna knew he was lying through his teeth—there was no way Aguado would just let them go after all that had happened. She had to think of something.

"I don't know what else to tell you. I honestly don't know where he is."

"You know, there are other ways I can find him," Aguado said. "The gringo assaulted a police officer and destroyed his vehicle. If I give that information to one of my contacts in the police department, every cop from here to Tijuana will be looking for him. And if they find him ..." He held his hands out, palms up. "I can't be sure what they'll do to him before taking him in. Do you understand what I'm saying?"

She understood the threat perfectly. But she also knew that if the police got ahold of Reynolds before Aguado, there was a chance the drive would fall into the wrong hands and Aguado would never allow that.

"Yes, I understand what you're saying. But I told your friend here I don't know where he is. He said he was going to run some errands while we were at the mall. That's all I know."

Aguado sighed loudly. "And what of this business with the DEA? Miguel tells me you had an agent's card in your purse."

"It's nothing. We went to the U.S. Consulate to see if they could get us expedited visas, that's all."

"I think you're lying, Ms. Rincon. The DEA doesn't handle immigration issues."

Anna squirmed a bit and lowered her voice. "We may have told them the cartel was chasing us."

"And what did your friend at the DEA have to say about that?"

"He said there was nothing they could do except get us the visas. That's it."

"I don't think you're telling me the whole truth," Aguado replied. "But lucky for you, we have time." He paused for effect, then continued. "Ms. Rincon, I *will* find the gringo and I *will* get my drive back. How that happens is up to you. Now I'll ask you one last time. Where. Is. The. Gringo?"

Anna lowered her head and looked at the floor. She was exhausted, scared, and tired of answering the same question over and over. In a half-whisper, she said, "I don't know where he is."

Aguado sighed again. "As you wish, Ms. Rincon."

He turned his attention to Alvarez. "Miguel, take them upstairs and put them in separate rooms until we find the gringo."

"Yes, Jefe," Alvarez replied.

———

The cot creaked and wobbled as Reynolds tossed and turned for the millionth time that night. He'd slept decently until two in the morning, but after that, for no more than thirty minutes at a time.

He groggily swung his legs over the side of the cot and stood up, stretching his arms in the air. The clock on the wall read seven-thirty, and he could hear a flurry of activity outside the conference room.

Reynolds quickly dressed and slipped on his shoes. He

rubbed his eyes and used the small sink to splash water on his face, trying to make himself look presentable.

As he exited the conference room, Reynolds spotted Agent Wilson hurrying in the down the hall, heading in the opposite direction.

"Agent Wilson!" he called after him.

The agent quickly turned. "Hey, good morning, Dillon."

"Good morning," Reynolds replied. "Is Agent Henderson here yet?"

"Yeah, I don't think he ever left. Last time I saw him, he was in his office. You're welcome to head that way if you like."

"Thanks," Reynolds said and began walking down the hall.

The smell of burned coffee permeated the air as he passed the small break room and approached Henderson's office.

"Knock, knock," Reynolds said, standing in the doorway.

Henderson looked up from his computer screen. "Hey, Dillon."

The agent looked tired. He had dark circles under his eyes, and he was wearing the same clothes as the previous day.

"Didn't make it out of here last night?" Reynolds said.

"Too much to do. Slept on the couch."

"Is everything in place for today?" Reynolds asked.

"Just got final approval from the Mexican Federal Police this morning. That was the last piece of the puzzle."

"So, what happens now?"

Henderson looked at his watch. "I'm going to brief the team at eight o'clock in the conference room. You'll need to be there. We'll go over the game plan one last time and then get to work. Pretty simple."

Reynolds coughed. "Yeah, simple alright. You're not the

one walking into a meeting with the world's most notorious drug dealer."

"Trust me Dillon, I would switch places with you in a heartbeat, but that's not the way this thing has to go down." He softened his voice. "You'll do fine. Just remember, if something goes sideways, be prepared to pivot. Check your surroundings for information and resources. Use your observations to create a plan, then make a backup plan. I promise, if you think quickly on your feet, we'll have Anna and Danny back in no time."

Reynolds nodded. "Thanks for the advice, but I'm hoping there will be less pivoting and more sticking to the plan."

"Just be prepared for anything. That's all I'm telling you."

Reynolds knew it was good advice. When he was a shortstop in Little League, his father had told him, "Always be on your toes. Always expect the ball to take a bad hop. Always expect the unexpected. If you're prepared for that, then nothing can surprise you."

The words rang truer now than ever.

"You mind if I grab a cup of coffee before heading back to the conference room?" Reynolds asked.

"Be my guest. Not sure it's going to be any good, though. It's been on since five."

Reynolds flashed his trademarked smile and said, "Then I'll *pivot* to a glass of water."

Henderson couldn't help laughing. "See? You're a pro already."

The coffee was indeed horrible, but Reynolds needed to wake up and he knew the jolt of caffeine would help so he forced down a cup.

Inside the conference room, the seats around the large table were now mostly filled with agents. Reynolds counted six from the DEA and two from the FBI.

The DEA agents were dressed in dark green fatigues and wore ballistic vests with the letters DEA embroidered on the front.

The two FBI agents were dressed in khaki pants and blue windbreakers that read FBI on the back in large yellow block letters.

All of them carried Glock nineteen sidearms on their hip. Reynolds watched as they chit-chatted about this or that, not seeming anxious or scared.

*How can these guys be so calm?* They were about to execute a raid on one of the most powerful criminals in the world, yet they acted like it was another day at the office.

"Good morning, ladies and gentlemen," Henderson said, breaking through his thoughts.

The agents muttered good morning and quieted themselves as Henderson took the seat at the head of the table, flanked by Wilson to his right.

"I want to go over the game plan for today's operation one more time. But first, let me introduce Dillon Reynolds. He'll be doing the heavy lifting today."

Reynolds nodded at the group seated around the table.

"Dillon Reynolds the baseball player?" said a hulking DEA agent they all referred to as Thor.

Reynolds grimaced. *Great, another baseball fan.*

"That's me," he said sheepishly.

"Didn't you hit like ten home runs in fifteen games your rookie season?" the agent asked.

"Guilty as charged."

The agent straightened in his chair. "Guilty, huh? You better be careful saying stuff like that around here."

Thor paused for a moment, then a grin cracked his solemn expression, and the others laughed in unison.

The agent to Reynolds' right put a hand on his shoulder. "We're just messing with you, partner. Welcome to the team." He had a thick southern accent that reminded Reynolds of Cledus from Smokey and the Bandit.

Henderson loudly cleared his throat. "Mind if we get back to work, people?"

As the room quieted again, Reynolds began briefing the team on the operation.

"The clock starts ticking when Dillon contacts Ed Hernandez. Dillon, I want you to tell Hernandez you won't proceed without proof that Anna and Danny are still alive."

Reynolds winced at Henderson's words. He didn't want to think of worst-case scenarios right now.

Henderson continued. "Once you have proof of life, tell Hernandez you will exchange the drive for Anna and Danny, but you will only give the drive to Aguado personally—no one else."

Reynolds nodded his understanding.

"Since there's no way to predict where Aguado will want to meet. We've scouted his home, known businesses, and those of his high-ranking associates using satellite photos and drone footage. We performed a risk assessment on each location to identify potential hazards and vulnerabilities, but the reality is, he may want to meet somewhere completely different, so we have to be prepared for anything."

He clicked a key on the laptop computer seated on the table in front of him, and the flatscreen television behind the conference table came to life. Henderson quickly went through potential issues with each location they'd scouted.

"This will be the most challenging locale."

Henderson pulled up a satellite photo of Aguado's compound outside Mazatlán.

The agent seated next to Reynolds whistled as he examined the aerial photos of the huge estate. "Whewee!" he drawled, toothpick hanging from one side of his mouth. "I thought you said crime don't pay Henderson. Looks like this ole boy is doin' alright."

"Don't get too jealous, Agent Boudreaux. After today, his prized possession will be soap on a rope."

The room exploded in raucous laughter for several minutes and finally died down when Henderson began speaking again.

"We'll split into two teams. Thor, you'll be leading the Alpha Team. Agent Boudreaux, you'll lead Bravo Team. Aguado's home is surrounded by a twelve-foot-tall stone wall, so Bravo Team will have to breach the perimeter behind the house without being seen by the cameras here and here."

He wiggled the cursor over two locations on the outside of the house. "There are two armed guards here ..." He pointed at the guardhouse. "... and here." He pointed at the overhang covering the front entry. "When I give the go signal, that means Aguado has taken the bait. Bravo Team will enter through the rear of the house and begin a sweep. Alpha Team will neutralize the guards at the gate, then move to the front of the house and take out the remaining two guards.

"Unfortunately, we can't predict how many men will be inside the house, but plan on at least Aguado and Alvarez. Now, I don't have to tell you surprise is our biggest advantage. We need to enter the house without incident so we can prevent this from becoming a hostage situation."

Henderson stared around the room. "Any questions?"

One of the FBI agents, a squatty woman with shoulder-length dirty blonde hair, asked, "What if it *does* become a hostage situation?"

"We'll cross that bridge if we come to it. Anything else?"

No other questions were asked.

"Alright then," Henderson said, rising from his chair.

"We're going to contact Mr. Hernandez. I'll update you when we have a location."

---

The upstairs bedroom was lavishly decorated, much like the rest of Aguado's estate. A massive chestnut wood bed sat against the far wall, its twisting pilasters inlaid with marble reliefs. Matching nightstands sat on either side of the bed, atop which a pair of gold lamps were placed, casting a warm light across two vases filled with bouquets of yellow roses.

Anna paced back and forth, wracking her brain for a workable plan—any plan, really. Alvarez had locked her in here last night before, presumably taking Danny to a different room in the massive house.

During the night, she had searched the room high and low for escape points but found none.

She was too far up on the second floor to escape through a window, and the door to the bedroom was locked with a heavy deadbolt. Escape seemed impossible. And even if she did manage to find a way out of the room, she'd still have to find Danny. They'd passed at least six or seven other doors on their way here—she'd never be able to check all of them without being discovered.

As the obstacles mounted, tears started to form at the corner of her eyes, and she began to breathe in heavy gasps. *Was this the end?* she thought. *Would they die in this place?*

She'd worked so hard to provide her son with a good life. All the hours spent in that stifling laundry, slaving away to make sure Danny didn't go without. The long nights she'd spent studying with him, ensuring he made the most of his education. And now that he finally had a chance to leave Villa Unión, to follow his dream of playing baseball, these men wanted to take that from him.

*No!* she thought angrily, and wiped away the tears from her face. These criminals would not take away Danny's dream. If she had to kill them herself, then so be it.

It calmed her. The thought of taking some small measure of control seemed to empower Anna, and slowly her breathing returned to normal. As she composed herself, she began to think tactically. If the plan was to kill them, she would need a weapon, something she could conceal until exactly the right moment.

Looking around the room, her gaze landed on one of the elegant glass vases filled with yellow roses. *That will do nicely.*

Quickly, she removed the flowers from the vase and placed it in the middle of the bed, wrapping it in the thick comforter. Next, she unplugged one of the heavy gold lamps and removed it from the nightstand. She took a deep breath and swung the base of the lamp down on the comforter with a grunt, shattering the vase.

The comforter muffled the sound well, but she still froze, waiting for Alvarez to storm into the bedroom.

But after a few long seconds, no one came. The house remained silent.

Carefully, Anna unwrapped the blanket and examined the shards of glass. As she had hoped, a medium-sized piece had broken off and now formed a narrow blade.

She picked it up and examined the splinter of glass. She imagined what it would feel like to plunge the shard into Alvarez's neck. The thought made her queasy. She had no experience with such violence and brutality, but she knew she had to push past the fear. There was nothing she wouldn't do to protect her son—even if it meant killing someone. She hoped the Lord would understand. She had no other choice.

Anna pulled back the comforter, exposing the crisp

white sheet beneath it. She cautiously held the razor-sharp piece of glass between her thumb and fingers and ran the edge along the sheet, cutting it into long strips. Next, she wrapped the strips of sheet around one end of the shard to form a padded handle.

When she was done, Anna admired her handiwork. She practiced stabbing and slicing, first with one grip, then another—trying to determine which would be more deadly.

After a few minutes of practice, she felt comfortable enough with the makeshift blade—as comfortable as she would ever get, she guessed. Anna carefully pocketed the knife and began picking up the remaining pieces of glass, then straightened the rest of the room, returning it to its original state.

With the room back in order, she slowly knelt by the bed and began to pray. She prayed for Danny. She prayed for herself. She prayed for Reynolds. And she prayed for forgiveness for what she was about to do.

As she whispered a quiet "Amen," a key jiggled in the lock, and she bolted upright.

*Now or never.*

She put a hand in her pocket, gripping the knife handle tightly as the door swung open.

---

Henderson closed the door to his office and motioned for Reynolds to take a seat. "Now remember, get proof of life first, then demand to personally give the drive to Aguado. Got it?"

Reynolds nodded as Henderson retrieved a cell phone from his desk drawer.

"For you." He slid a new phone across his desk. "We've installed a surveillance program on it, so we'll know where you are, who you're talking to, and what you're talking about. We also uploaded a list of contacts and a bunch of apps, so the phone looks legit if anyone searches it. Oh, and if you get into trouble, click on the Instagram app."

"What, do you want me to post a selfie with Aguado?" Reynolds quipped.

"Funny, but no. It's not actually Instagram. When you open the app, it will send an SOS directly to me, so I'll know you're in trouble."

"I like the selfie idea better," Reynolds said with a wry smile.

"I'm glad you've got your sense of humor back. You ready?"

Reynolds took a deep breath. "Ready as I'll ever be."

"Ed's phone number is in the contacts," Henderson said.

Reynolds pulled up the contact list and clicked the number for Ed Hernandez, then put the phone on speaker.

"Ed Hernandez," the voice on the other end answered.

Reynolds cleared his throat. "Ed, it's Dillon."

There was a long pause before Hernandez replied, "Dillon, I thought I'd heard the last of you. What's going on? Where are you?"

"Listen Ed, I'm going to cut to the chase. I know you're working with the cartel. I saw the loans on your desk, and I know who Eldorado Finance is."

Another long pause.

"Dillon, it's more complicated than that. I..."

Reynolds cut over him. "It's not, Ed. What you do is your business, but what you're doing to those families is wrong and you know it."

"Is that what you called to tell me?" Hernandez said.

"No, it's not. I called to tell you I want to make a deal with Aguado."

"I don't have any pull with Aguado."

"But you know how to contact Miguel Alvarez, don't you?"

"And what would you have me tell Mr. Alvarez?"

"I want you to tell him I want to make a trade. The drive for Anna and Danny."

"What are you talking about, Dillon?"

Reynolds raised his voice, "You know exactly what I'm talking about, Ed. The cartel has kidnapped Anna and Danny to get to me so they can have their damn drive."

Hernandez sounded confused. "I ... I had no idea."

"Can you help me or not Ed?" Reynolds eyed Henderson, who gave him a thumbs up.

"I'll see what I can do."

"Good. Two more things. First, I want proof that Anna and Danny are alive. And second, I will only give the drive to Aguado himself—no one else."

"You sure you know what you're doing, Dillon?" Hernandez asked.

"Yes, I'm sure. Now, do you understand my terms?"

"I understand."

"Good. You can reach me at this number."

Reynolds ended the call.

"Pretty good," Henderson said. "Now we wait."

## CHAPTER 20

Alvarez and Zapata sat in the study, discussing plans for the manufacture and distribution of Azúcar when Alvarez's phone buzzed. He looked at the screen, then looked at Aguado. "Ed Hernandez."

Aguado nodded and Alvarez clicked open the call. "Sí."

"Miguel, Dillon Reynolds just called me."

Alvarez's eyes narrowed, and he set the phone on Aguado's desk, then clicked the speaker button. "What did he want?"

"He said he wants to make a deal. The drive for the woman and the kid."

"So, he knows we have them?" Alvarez replied.

"Yes, he said he wanted proof they were alive. After that, he said he would only give the drive to Mr. Aguado personally."

"Stay on the line," Alvarez said and hit the mute button.

"What do you think, Jefe?"

"I think Mr. Reynolds is a fool," he grumbled. "How does he know we won't just kill him when we have the drive?"

Alvarez shrugged. "How do we know he didn't make a copy of the drive?"

Aguado thought for a moment. "It seems we'll have to trust each other," he said warily. "Have Hernandez tell Mr. Reynolds we'll get his proof of life. When he's satisfied, I want Hernandez to meet him at the Baseball Academy, where they'll await further instructions. And Miguel, tell him if we even so much as think a DEA agent is following him, he'll never see the woman or the kid ever again."

Alvarez nodded and took the call off mute, relaying the instructions to Hernandez.

With the call complete, Aguado looked at Alvarez with a solemn stare. "Miguel, I want Hernandez to bring the gringo here."

He turned to Zapata. "Rafael, go get the chemist. We'll need him to verify the formula is correct."

"Yes, Jefe." Zapata quickly stood and left the room.

Aguado turned his attention back to Alvarez. "Miguel, go get the gringo his proof of life."

As Alvarez readied himself to leave the study, Aguado called after him. "And Miguel, when we have the drive, none of them walk out of here. Am I clear?"

"Yes, Jefe," Alvarez replied.

---

Reynolds and Henderson remained in the office after the call to Ed Hernandez. The minutes seemed like hours as they waited for a callback. Finally, after nearly half an hour of staring at the phone, the call came through.

"Dillon, I got ahold of Alvarez," Hernandez's voice said over the speaker.

"And?" Reynolds pressed.

"And he agreed to your terms. Can I text the phone you're calling from?"

"Yes."

"Okay, I'm sending proof of life now."

Reynolds clicked on the text from Hernandez. It contained two photos. One of a scared, drained-looking Anna holding up a piece of paper with today's date and time crudely scribbled in black marker. The second photo was similar, this one with Danny holding up the same piece of paper.

Reynolds' blood boiled as he slid the phone to Henderson. He could see the fear in both Anna's and Danny's eyes, and he cursed himself for not being there for them.

The DEA agent studied the photos momentarily and gave a thumbs up.

"Okay, Ed," Reynolds said. "Now, what about the meeting with Aguado?"

"Alvarez said for you to meet me at the Academy. When you're here, he'll send instructions on where to meet."

Reynolds looked to Henderson and held his arms out, palms up. Henderson mouthed the word "Dammit," then reluctantly nodded for Reynolds to accept the meeting at the Academy.

"Okay, Ed. I can meet you at the Academy, but it's going to take me some time to get there. Can we meet at four this afternoon?"

"Text me when you're here."

"Alright." Reynolds ended the call.

Henderson leaned back in his chair and sighed. "I was hoping they wouldn't play this game. I guarantee once they give the instructions where to meet, they'll want the meeting to take place quickly, which won't give us much time to prepare."

"At least we know it'll be somewhere in, or at least near, Mazatlán, if that's the case."

"True," Henderson said. "We'll have plenty of time to go

over the locations around Mazatlán on the way there. Let's mount up."

Henderson led the way back to the conference room to brief the other agents. "We've got our first location."

"*First* location?" asked the agent nicknamed Thor.

"Yes. They've requested that Dillon meet with Ed Hernandez at the Baseball Academy in Mazatlán."

He could hear the group collectively groan, knowing that a seven-hour drive was ahead of them.

"Once Dillon gets to the Academy," Henderson continued, "Alvarez will send instructions on where the meeting with Aguado will take place. Keep in mind, once they send the location, they'll want to meet quickly, so we won't have much time to prepare."

The agents nodded. "Reynolds can ride with me in the van. I'll drop him off a few miles from the Academy and have him take a cab the rest of the way so as not to arouse suspicion. The rest of you will take B.O.B. Any questions?"

There were none, and the group began filing out of the conference room toward the gated lot outside the Consulate building.

"What's a B.O.B.?" Reynolds asked.

"It's … a technical term." Henderson replied with the hint of a smile.

"What?" Reynolds pressed.

"It stands for Big Ole Bitch. B-O-B. Get it?"

"Do I even want to know why it's called that?" Reynolds asked.

"Well, it's officially called the Mobile Tactical Operations Center, but Agent Boudreaux thought that was too long, so he came up with B.O.B."

Reynolds narrowed his eyes.

"It's a specialized vehicle we had outfitted with bulletproof glass, run flat tires and armored panels that can withstand a fifty-caliber round. It's big enough that we can store extra weapons, ammunition, and other fun toys the DEA gives us."

As they walked through the lot, Henderson pointed at a large box truck wrapped in branding for a plumbing company—*La Casita del Plomero.*

"That's B.O.B.," he said. "Looks like every other plumbing truck in Mexico—except there's a surprise inside. Kind of like a box of Cracker Jacks."

Reynolds eyed him with a sideways glance. "If that's you trying to be funny, I think you should stick to the whole law enforcement thing."

Henderson chuckled. "You're probably right."

As they continued, Henderson approached a white Ram ProMaster van, wrapped with the same plumber's branding as B.O.B.

"This is us," he said.

Reynolds opened the passenger door and climbed in. A thin metal wall separated the cab of the van from the cargo area, leaving room for two bucket seats and a narrow center console between them.

Mounted to the console was a laptop computer and what looked like a CB radio. Henderson clicked it on and picked up the handheld microphone. "Radio check. Radio check. S.A.M. to B.O.B. Over."

The small speaker crackled to life. "S.A.M. this is B.O.B. We read you loud and clear. Over."

"S.A.M.?" Reynolds asked. "Another pet name?"

"Nah, this one's pretty straightforward," Henderson replied. "Surveillance and monitoring. S-A-M."

Reynolds shrugged. These guys sure loved their acronyms.

Henderson started the van and eased it through the gated exit, followed closely by B.O.B.

As they drove, Henderson gave Reynolds pointers on everything from how to best position himself when walking into a room to self-defense tricks like the palm heel strike and front kick.

Reynolds pored through surveillance photos on the computer, with Henderson pointing out escape routes and potential pinch points to avoid.

When they tired of the business at hand, the conversation turned to Reynolds' brief time in the Major leagues, his relationship with Anna and Danny and finally to Henderson and his career in the DEA.

Finally, after seven long hours, the small caravan rolled to a stop in the parking lot of a roadside hotel. They were approximately fifteen minutes from the Academy and Reynolds couldn't wait to get out of the stuffy van.

"You'll need to take a cab from here," Henderson said. "We can't risk Hernandez seeing the trucks. But don't worry, we'll be right behind you. I'll be tracking you through your phone and a dedicated satellite the DEA dialed up for this mission. We'll have eyes on you at all times."

Reynolds nodded, and Henderson handed him the small USB drive containing the virus then patted Reynolds on the shoulder. "And remember, if you get into trouble, just click the Instagram icon. We'll be there within minutes, if not seconds."

Reynolds took a deep breath and opened the door, then stepped out of the van. Before closing the door, he said, "Life's funny, isn't it?"

"How's that?" Henderson replied.

"A few months ago, making a fielding error or swinging at a bad pitch was the most stressful thing in my life." He paused. "Kind of puts things into perspective."

Henderson chuckled. "Perspective can be a valuable tool, Dillon. Remember that."

The door to the bedroom opened, and Alvarez strode in holding a piece of paper. "Hold this up," he said, not offering an explanation.

Anna looked at the paper. It had today's date and what she assumed was the current time written on it.

As Alvarez reached to hand her the paper, she slowly began pulling the knife from her pocket. She eyed the side of his neck where she would plunge the blade. The man wouldn't know what had hit him.

Then she stopped.

Why would Alvarez want her to hold up the paper with the date and time on it? she wondered.

*Unless ... someone wanted proof they were still alive.*

It hit her—someone was coming for them! She was right about Dillon. She knew he would never give up on them.

Anna quickly released her grip on the knife and took the paper, holding it in front of her.

Alvarez removed a phone from his pocket and snapped a quick picture before snatching the paper back and leaving the room.

Alone again, Anna dared to feel a sliver of hope. Maybe there was still a chance they'd get out of this place.

After the visit from Alvarez, the time ticked away slowly. She watched for hours through the window as the sun descended in the western sky. She wondered what was going on downstairs. Why were their rescuers taking so long? Or had she misread the situation? Would there be no rescue? Had she missed her chance to kill Alvarez?

Before her thoughts could spiral out of control, she heard keys jiggle in the lock and turned to see Alvarez in the doorway.

"Come with me," he said.

She approached the doorway and squeezed past the unmoving Alvarez.

"Downstairs," he growled, following her a bit too closely.

She navigated the grand staircase and stopped in the entryway.

"This way," Alvarez instructed.

The man led her back to the study where Aguado had interrogated her yesterday.

Inside the room, Aguado sat behind a large desk while a ruddy-faced American with a receding hairline sat on a sofa across the room. She recognized the American. It was the man that had crashed into their dinner table—Felix Martin.

"Sit down," Alvarez ordered.

Anna took a seat opposite Martin and stared back at Aguado with a cold gaze. She turned her attention as Danny entered the study, followed by Zapata, who closed the door behind him.

Danny stared at his mother, then Martin, before seating himself between the two.

With everyone seated, Aguado began. "Ms. Rincon, it appears your friend Mr. Reynolds has chosen to do the right thing. He'll be here any minute to give us our drive. What I want from you and your son is complete cooperation. If you don't cause any trouble, I'll send you on your way once I've verified the drive is authentic. Do you understand?"

She understood perfectly. Aguado was a brutal killer and would almost certainly execute them when he had the drive in his possession. They knew too much about his operation and the Azúcar. There was simply no way he was just going to "send them on their way."

"Yes, I understand."

Anna was suddenly glad she still had the knife in her pocket—as well as the element of surprise. She began to form a plan.

When Reynolds arrived and Aguado's attention was focused on the drive, she would stab Alvarez in the neck with the glass blade. Hopefully, Reynolds would follow suit and disarm Zapata before Aguado could react.

The wildcard here was Felix Martin. The guy didn't look like much. He also didn't seem to be very fond of Aguado. She quickly decided he wasn't a threat. But if he tried to intervene, she would deal with him as well.

She thought about Danny. *What if he tried to get involved? What if he got hurt?* She forced herself not to entertain the possibility. Danny was big and strong. He could handle himself. Besides, the odds were not in their favor, and they would need all the help they could get.

She turned at a soft knocking coming from the door.

Aguado sneered, "They're here."

---

The small green and white taxi pulled up in front of the Academy.

Reynolds handed the driver a few bills and stepped out onto the sidewalk. He'd spent so many hours here, met so many friends, had so many good memories inside that building. For obvious reasons, he'd resigned himself to never coming back. But now that he was standing in front of the Academy, he realized how much he missed this place.

A car horn somewhere on the street brought him back to the present, and he reached for the phone in his pocket. Taking a quick look around, he scanned the sidewalk for anything that seemed out of place. Satisfied there was no danger, Reynolds clicked the number for Ed Hernandez and put the phone to his ear.

"Dillon, are you here?"

"Yes, I'm out front."

"I'll tell the guard to let you in. Come up to my office."

As Reynolds approached the small white stucco guard house, the gate beside it slid open and the guard nodded for him to enter.

He made his way to the entrance of the building and upstairs to a waiting Ed Hernandez.

"Hola, Amigo," Hernandez greeted him cautiously.

"Ed," was all Reynolds could manage in reply.

"Come in and close the door."

Reynolds did as he was instructed, taking a seat in one of the guest chairs as Hernandez dialed Alvarez.

"He's here at the Academy," Hernandez said into the phone, then listened carefully and began jotting something down on a piece of paper in front of him.

When he hung up the phone, Hernandez looked across the desk at Reynolds. "They want to meet in thirty minutes."

"Where?" Reynolds questioned.

"Don't know. Alvarez just gave me an address. It's about twenty-five minutes north of here."

"We'd better get going then," Reynolds replied.

Hernandez stood from his chair and opened a drawer beneath the glass desktop. When he lifted his hand, Reynolds saw he held a polished chrome Desert Eagle pistol. He quickly slipped the weapon into his waistband and covered it with his shirt.

"You really think you're going to need that?" Reynolds said.

"You never know, amigo." Hernandez replied and headed for the door.

Reynolds could only shake his head as he stared at the man he had once considered a mentor. Now all he could see was a crooked loan shark and a cartel lackey.

Hernandez led the way down to the lobby and out the front entrance of the Academy. In the parking lot, his Range

Rover gleamed in the afternoon sun. The site of the expensive SUV made Reynolds wonder how many poor families the man had fleeced to pay for it. It sickened him.

They rode in silence as Hernandez navigated through the evening traffic. Reynolds' mind raced in anticipation of the meeting with Aguado. He thought back to the photos of Anna and Danny holding the paper in front of them. They both looked so scared and helpless.

*Hold on just a little longer,* Reynolds thought. *Just a little longer.*

Eventually, the SUV slowed and turned off the highway down a narrow dirt road. The Ranger Rover bumped down the drive, kicking up a trail of dust behind it until they reached a massive gate.

Two men armed with AR-15 rifles emerged from a large guardhouse on the right side of the gate. One of them approached the vehicle and motioned for Hernandez to roll down the window.

"We're here to see Alvarez," Hernandez said to the guard.

The man nodded, and the enormous gate swung open.

Hernandez steered the SUV off the dirt road and down a winding cobblestone driveway, finally parking behind a black Cadillac Escalade.

Reynolds got out of the SUV and stared at the house. It had to have been over twenty thousand square feet, looking more like a hotel than a private residence. The massive estate was styled in classic Spanish architecture, with white stucco walls, a low pitched, terra-cotta clay tile roof, and a set of hand carved wooden double doors guarding the entrance.

The second floor of the building was dotted with multi-paned windows, each with its own small wrought-iron balcony that overlooked the manicured gardens below.

Much like the front gate, two men armed with AR-15 rifles stood under the port cochere guarding the front of the home.

As Hernandez and Reynolds approached the front door, one of the guards, a tall man wearing Aviator sunglasses, stepped forward and put a hand on Reynolds' chest. "Is this the gringo?" he asked Hernandez.

"Yes, Dillon Reynolds," Hernandez replied.

The guard eyed Reynolds and said something to his counterpart in Spanish. The other man grabbed Reynolds by the arm and roughly shoved him against the stucco wall. He began a pat down, starting at the feet and stopping when he felt the phone in Reynolds' front pocket. He removed it and continued the pat down, eventually discovering the USB drive in Reynolds' other pocket.

He held up the drive for Aviator glasses to inspect.

"Aquí," Aviator demanded. He examined the small piece of hardware before handing it back to Reynolds.

Reynolds quickly noted that Hernandez was not subject to a pat down. *Looks you're real chummy with these assholes, aren't you Ed?*

Aviator motioned for his partner to open the entry door and led Hernandez and Reynolds into the massive estate.

Even Hernandez, who was somewhat used to being around money and power, was impressed with the sheer volume of the grand entry. The soaring ceilings, elegant staircases, and lavish décor—it all seemed so over the top. Purposely so, he guessed.

Aviator led the small group left through the entry and down a hallway toward a large set of arched wooden doors. He knocked lightly and moments later one of the doors creaked open, revealing a smirking Miguel Alvarez.

"Mr. Reynolds," he said. "You're a hard man to find."

## CHAPTER 21

Both plumbing trucks followed the Range Rover from a distance. Just far enough not to be seen by Hernandez, but close enough to converge quickly if something went wrong.

After dropping Reynolds in the hotel parking lot, Henderson had taken a seat in the back of the surveillance van while Wilson took over driving duties, following the little green and white taxi until it reached the Academy. The convoy had parked across the street at the Oxxo and waited until Hernandez and Reynolds emerged from the building and drove out of the parking lot.

Now, as they sped north on the highway, Henderson pulled on a wireless headset and pulled the microphone near his mouth. "B.O.B. this is S.A.M. Do you copy?"

"Copy S.A.M."

"Looks like they're headed to Aguado's compound," Henderson said into the mike.

"Roger that S.A.M."

"Good. Let's do this just like we discussed this morning."

"Affirmative," came the radio reply.

Henderson stared at the live satellite feed on the screen

in front of him. The Range Rover had slowed and turned down a dirt road leading to the compound.

Seconds later, Wilson passed the dirt road and pulled the van to a stop on the side of the highway, followed shortly after by B.O.B.

The narrow dirt road was a straight shot to Aguado's compound, and the plumbing trucks would be spotted well before they could make it to the gate. So, Henderson had instructed the team to park on the highway and approach the target on foot, navigating their way through the thick vegetation surrounding the compound.

As agents poured out of the back of B.O.B. and disappeared into the trees, Wilson slid open the van door and climbed into the back. The wall opposite the sliding door was lined with two large computer monitors, under which sat a bevy of digital video and audio recorders, GPS devices and signal interception equipment that allowed the van to capture digital communications like cell phone calls and texts.

While Henderson studied the live satellite feed on the monitor in front of him, Wilson fired up the neighboring screen. He clicked the small skull and crossbones icon in the corner of the monitor and pulled up the same dashboard he'd demonstrated in the Greek restaurant.

Wilson donned a serious look and turned toward Henderson. "For those about to rock ..." he said, pulling on a matching headset. "... we salute you." He turned back to his monitor and fired a crisp salute at the screen.

Henderson slowly shook his head, quickly curtailing the smile that had begun to form at the corners of his lips. The kid was growing on him.

The monitor in front of Henderson glowed with green dots, moving through the foliage. The dots represented the digital tracking beacons worn by each agent. The beacons transmitted a unique signal to the DEA satellite, which would provide precise location information as well as access to the agent's body cam.

Henderson watched intently as the Bravo Team flanked the compound to the north and south while the Alpha Team waited in ambush for the two guards at the gate. Everyone was in place.

He clicked a button on the keyboard in front of him and the screen split into two halves—the green dots on one side, a monitoring program for Reynolds' phone on the other. Henderson could see that Reynolds had stopped at the front entrance for a few minutes, and was now entering the house.

The audio feed from the phone crackled in his headset. At first it was muffled, then Henderson heard a man call out, "Aquí."

There was more muffled noise, then a creak, most likely the sound of the front door opening.

A few seconds later, a different voice came through the headset: "Mr. Reynolds, you're a hard man to find."

―――――

The man standing in the doorway was small—maybe five and a half feet tall with slicked back hair, a gaudy western shirt and alligator skin cowboy boots.

*Surely this can't be Miguel Alvarez,* Reynolds thought. He looked more like a hokey character out of a movie than a cartel enforcer.

"Let them in, Miguel," a voice called from behind the small man.

Alvarez gestured for Reynolds and Hernandez to enter, then took Reynolds' phone from the guard. As the guard returned to the front of the house, Alvarez closed the door to the study and quietly twisted the lock.

"Gentlemen, so good of you to make it," Aguado's voice boomed. "Please, take a seat."

He gestured to a group of antique chairs, where Zapata was already seated.

"Beg your pardon, Jefe, but do you mind if I stand?" Hernandez asked, pointing at his spine. "Bad back."

Aguado shrugged. "Just stay out of the way."

Hernandez immediately took two steps back. "Yes, Jefe."

As he sat down, Reynolds shot Anna a nervous glance, then turned to Danny and winked, trying to assure the boy that everything would be alright. Next, he turned and looked at the man seated next to them—Felix Martin. He was surprised to see the guy was still alive after the two cartel goons had chased him out of the restaurant.

*Good,* Reynolds thought. *One more witness to testify against Aguado.*

Alvarez walked to Reynolds. "The drive." he demanded.

Reynolds produced the drive from his pocket and handed it to Alvarez who returned to Aguado's desk and placed both Reynolds' phone and the USB drive in front of Aguado.

"I assume there aren't any copies of the drive, Mr. Reynolds?" Aguado questioned.

"This is the only one." Reynolds replied.

"Mr. Martin," Aguado barked, holding up the drive. "Is this the drive you put in the envelope?"

Martin eyed the drive. It was gray and purple and looked similar enough. "Uh, yes, I think so."

"I want you to verify the formula is correct. Use my computer."

A shot of adrenaline surged through Reynolds' veins. *This might actually work,* he thought.

Martin pulled himself off the couch and nervously approached Aguado's desk. The man rose from his chair and motioned for the chemist to sit.

Reynolds watched closely as Martin inserted the drive into the side of Aguado's laptop with trembling fingers.

Martin paused for a moment, then clicked something on the screen.

The room collectively jumped as a tinny laugh began to emanate from the speakers on the laptop. The noise pierced the silence of the room as the impish cackle assaulted their eardrums.

Martin quickly pressed the volume button on the computer. Nothing. It wouldn't stop.

As the noise echoed through the room, Martin stared at the screen in horror. The monitor was now filled with an animated picture of a blonde woman in a bikini holding a surfboard. A speech bubble popped up near her mouth: "U dun been hacked."

He looked frantically at Aguado. "I don't know what's happening," he shouted over the din.

Alvarez and Zapata visibly tensed as Aguado furiously stomped back to his desk.

Seeing the screen, he turned to Reynolds with a piercing stare and bellowed, "What the hell is this?"

---

Inside the van, Agent Wilson watched the screen light up as if it had been plugged into a fire hydrant full of data. Aguado's deepest, darkest secrets now streamed over the internet and landed on a DEA hard drive, in the back of the van.

"We got him!" Wilson yelled, and patted Henderson on the back.

"All teams, we're a go!" Henderson barked into the

microphone. "They're in the southwest corner of the house. Ground floor. Go now!"

Two snipers from the Alpha Team lay in a prone position on the jungle floor, their weapons trained on the men in the guardhouse. When the go signal came, they immediately neutralized both men with a pair of well-aimed shots from suppressed Remington 700 sniper rifles. The remaining team members quickly entered the guardhouse, where they scanned the interior of the compound for threats.

While Alpha Team dealt with the guards at the gate, Bravo Team quietly breached the perimeter wall at the rear of the property and now crept out of view of the security cameras. They crouched low and inched around a sparkling blue swimming pool toward a set of French doors at the rear of the house.

The entry gate was far enough away that the two men standing guard at the main house hadn't heard the commotion at the front of the property. The extra time allowed the members of Alpha Team to take up firing positions behind a mountainous stone waterfall in the center of a sprawling garden, opposite the front door of the house.

Once again, the Alpha Team snipers fired in unison, dropping both guards where they stood. As the round struck his forehead, a cigarette fell from the mouth of the tall man wearing Aviator glasses and bounced off the cobblestone, sparking orange embers as it rolled.

"Go! Go!" whispered one of the agents into his headset, and the others emerged from their positions behind the waterfall, quickly making their way under the port cochere.

Henderson watched the glowing dots as the agents converged on the home from the front and rear. He could see Bravo Team had already gained entry and was carefully sweeping each room on the way to Reynolds' location.

Seconds later, Alpha Team had also made their way inside and had now positioned themselves at various points in the entryway.

"Alpha Team," Henderson said into the microphone.

"Copy," whispered Thor.

"Reynolds is approximately seventy-five feet to the southwest."

The agent looked southwest down the entryway and to his left, down a long hall. A pair of arched wooden doors sat at the end of the corridor, now the only thing standing between them and their target.

As they crept toward the doors, Thor caught a streak of motion from the second-floor balcony. A flash of white moved quickly behind them, then another in the opposite direction. *We're being flanked,* he thought.

Before he could call out the threat, gunshots rained down from above like a swarm of angry hornets. Bullets lanced into the floor, sending stone shrapnel in every direction. Dust and smoke clouded the room, eventually forming a gauzy curtain between the agents and their attackers.

It was just the right amount of cover. Retreating through the haze, the agents from Alpha Team quickly backed away from the hallway and took refuge behind a pair of towering stone columns on either side of the entry.

As the haze thinned, the agents could see the cartel shooters had taken up prone positions on the balcony, giving them a greater field of fire and reducing their profiles to razor thin targets.

The agents were effectively pinned down in the entryway—with nowhere to go.

Thor mulled retreating out the front door. It was an option. But there could easily be another ambush waiting for them outside. *No, the right move was to stay here and wait for Bravo Team,* he thought. At least here in the entryway, they had some small measure of cover.

"Bravo Team, this is Alpha Team. We're experiencing heavy resistance from two shooters on the second-floor balcony. We're pinned down in the entryway."

"Copy Alpha Team," Boudreaux replied. "On our way."

Bravo Team crept through the house, scanning each room as they worked their way through the massive residence. They moved quietly through the kitchen into a wide hallway separating the front of the house from the rear.

As they approached the opening from the hallway to the entry, Boudreaux whispered into the mike. "Alpha Team. What's your position?"

"We're pinned down behind two columns at the front of the entry. There's a pair of shooters above us on the second-floor balcony."

"Roger that, Alpha Team," Boudreaux twanged. "Your white knight is on the way."

He removed a flash bang from a pocket on his ballistic vest and motioned for another agent to do the same. Then he made an underhand throwing motion and pointed to the balcony directly above them.

He held up three fingers and began a countdown as the agents inched their way under the balcony. When the countdown reached zero, the agents lobbed the flash bangs over the railing and beat a hasty retreat down the hall.

The men on the balcony recoiled and covered their heads as the concussion grenades exploded in white hot light, sending waves of searing pain through their optic nerves and blinding them. The shock wave slammed through their bodies, compressing their organs, shattering their ear drums.

As the shooters stumbled about the balcony, utterly

disoriented, Alpha Team began firing on their positions, dropping one then the other.

---

"I asked you a question!" Aguado roared over the eerie laughter that spouted from the laptop. He picked up the computer and hurled it against the marble fireplace, sending electronic shrapnel in a dozen directions.

As the noise from the destroyed computer faded, another replaced it—gun shots.

A long, continuous barrage of automatic rifle fire came from down the hall toward the entryway. The shots were immediately followed by a shorter, more concise volley. The back and forth continued for a few long seconds, tailing off to a single shot here or there.

It sounded as if the two sides had come to an impasse.

As the firing died down, Alvarez removed his weapon and trained it on Danny. Zapata followed suit, pointing his nine-millimeter at Reynolds.

"If someone comes through that door, kill them!" Aguado roared.

Before Alvarez or Zapata could react, Aguado heard the metallic click of the hammer being thumbed back on a polished chrome Desert Eagle pistol.

"I don't think so, Mr. Aguado," Ed Hernandez said. He stood calmly behind Aguado, holding the pistol against the back of the drug lord's head.

"What the hell are you doing, Hernandez?" Aguado hissed.

Hernandez's face was somber. "Something I should have done a long time ago. Now tell your men to put down their guns."

"I'd rather die," Aguado said between clenched teeth. "Miguel, Rafael, if I die, everyone dies."

Alvarez nodded and pressed the gun hard against Danny's chest.

During the commotion, Anna had slowly removed the shard of glass from her pocket and now held it by her side, concealed against her leg.

Felix Martin eyed the weapon as Anna wrapped her fingers around the cloth handle. She noticed his gaze, and shot the chemist a fiery look that said, *Keep your mouth shut.*

Message received, Martin hunched back on the sofa and inched farther away from Anna.

She quickly measured the situation. With Danny seated between her and Alvarez, it would be difficult to hit her target. She would need a distraction to close the distance between them—but what?

At that moment, two loud explosions burst from the entryway to the house, blasts in quick succession.

The diversion allowed Anna time to jump off the couch and lunge at Alvarez, stabbing through the air with the razor-sharp fragment of glass. Alvarez raised a hand to deflect the blow and managed to prevent the blade from completely piercing his neck. Instead of penetrating deep into the man's flesh, as Anna had planned, the knife sunk only a quarter of an inch.

But as Alvarez continued the defensive motion, his forearm forced the blade hard across his skin, slashing across his neck and severing his carotid artery. The gash spewed hot spatters of blood across the front of Anna's shirt as Danny watched in shock.

Alvarez dropped the gun and clutched futilely at his neck, trying to stop the bleeding.

*Time to pivot,* Reynolds thought.

As Alvarez gurgled and coughed, Reynolds leapt from

his chair and put a heavy shoulder into Zapata, who had been staring at Alvarez in disbelief. Both men toppled over Zapata's chair, with Reynolds landing on his back behind his opponent.

Reynolds quickly rolled to a knee and pounced on Zapata, trying to straddle his chest so he could rain down vicious elbows like he'd done with the crooked cop. Instead, Zapata threw a sharp knee into Reynolds' stomach. The blow forced the wind from his lungs, causing him to double over in pain.

As Reynolds gasped and wheezed, trying to recapture his breath, Zapata gathered himself and launched a fierce right hook to the side of his head. The blow hit him square on the temple, causing tiny flashes of bright light to speckle his vision. Milliseconds later, the flashes of light faded, replaced by a slowly drawn curtain of blackness that draped over Reynolds and dragged him downward, into unconsciousness.

Zapata stared at the motionless Reynolds, then around the room, eyes frantically searching for his gun. As he spotted the weapon, Danny charged at him, knocking Zapata back towards the set of antique chairs. The two landed in a heap on the floor. Instinctively, Zapata sat up and quickly wrapped a powerful arm around Danny's neck, squeezing the boy's airway with bone-crushing pressure.

"Stop!" Anna called. "You're going to kill him!"

"Get me the gun!" Zapata yelled at her.

"No!" Hernandez yelled at Anna. "Don't do it!"

Without a second thought, she ran to the gun. Her hands trembled as she picked it up and began to hand it back to Zapata.

As he reached out to take the weapon, the doors at the front of the study burst open. Agents streamed into the room, guns pointed in every direction.

Thor leveled his rifle at Hernandez. "Drop the gun!"

Hernandez quickly complied and held his hands in the air.

Agent Boudreaux scanned the room and spotted Zapata holding Danny in a chokehold. "Let the boy go!" he said.

"Fuck you, cabron!" Zapata spat back, tucking his head close behind Danny's. "You take one more step and I'll break his neck."

Danny stopped squirming and looked at Boudreaux with panic-stricken eyes.

Boudreaux froze. "Take it easy, partner."

"I want a car waiting for me outside now!" Zapata demanded. "Once I'm down the road, I'll let the kid out."

"I reckon that's a pretty fair offer there, partner. If you'd be so kind as to look at *Agent Thor* over there, he'll be happy to assist you." Boudreaux put a little extra emphasis on the words 'Agent Thor,' but directed Zapata's gaze instead to the squatty FBI agent on his right.

Zapata turned his head to look at the agent and, in doing so, exposed the side of his face to Agent Thor, who was positioned directly in front of him.

Thor gently squeezed the trigger on the AR-15 and sent a perfectly placed round of .556 ammunition into the side of Zapata's head. The man's skull nearly split in two and his body immediately went limp.

Danny dislodged Zapata's lifeless arm from around his neck and released himself from the chokehold. He sucked in huge gasps of air as he ran to Anna and wrapped his arms tightly around her.

"It's ok now, Mijo," she whispered. "We're safe."

Thor called into his mic, "All clear. Target secured."

"I'll need you to drop the weapon, ma'am," Boudreaux said softly.

Anna turned and handed him the gun. "Dillon. He's hurt."

Boudreaux quickly knelt over Reynolds and placed two fingers on his neck. The pulse was strong. "What happened?"

"He was fighting with that man." She pointed to Zapata's lifeless body. "And he got punched in the head, here." She pointed to her temple.

As she explained what had happened, Reynolds began to stir. His eyes fluttered, and he rolled on his side.

"Easy, partner," Boudreaux instructed.

Reynolds opened his eyes wide and tried to blink away the cobwebs. "Wha ... what happened?" He strained to sit up.

Boudreaux put a hand on his shoulder to steady him. "Sounds like you got in one heck of a fight with that ole' boy." He pointed to Zapata.

"Did I do that to him?" Reynolds asked, looking at the pool of blood around Zapata's motionless body.

"That right there is the handiwork of Agent Thor," Boudreaux explained. "But you gave us a good head start, partner."

As Reynolds collected himself and the agents began processing the room, Henderson and Wilson strode into the study.

Wilson immediately approached Thor, now rummaging through Aguado's desk. "Did we miss anything?"

The hulking agent simply snorted and returned to the desk drawer.

"I'll take that as a no," Wilson replied, then headed to where Henderson was questioning a handcuffed Ed Hernandez.

Anna could see the restraints on Hernandez's wrists as

Henderson questioned him. "Excuse me? Agent Henderson?"

He turned. "Yes, Ms. Rincon?"

"This man should not be in handcuffs. He helped us. Without Mr. Hernandez, we'd probably be dead right now."

Henderson turned back to Hernandez and raised an eyebrow. "Is that so?"

Hernandez shrugged and turned his gaze to the floor.

Anna continued. "Aguado told his men to shoot us if you came into the room and that's when Mr. Hernandez pulled a gun on him."

"She's right, Henderson." A still-dazed Reynolds approached the group and continued. "We owe this man our lives."

"Alright, alright." Henderson conceded and began removing the cuffs.

Reynolds turned to Hernandez. "Thanks Ed. And I'm sorry about ..."

Hernandez cut him off before he could offer the apology. "You were right, Dillon. Issuing the loans to those families was awful. I knew half of them wouldn't be able to pay back a dime—but I did it, anyway. Looks like I've got some amends to make."

Reynolds smiled. "I would agree. In fact, it sounds like you'll be busy for the foreseeable future. Maybe I can hang out a while longer—you know, look after the Academy while you're running around righting wrongs."

A wide grin emerged from behind Ed's handlebar mustache. "I think your room is still available, amigo."

# CHAPTER 22

The following morning, Henderson requested that Reynolds, Anna and Danny meet him at the U.S. Consulate in Mazatlán for a debriefing.

Since Anna's apartment was a wreck, Henderson had arranged for the group to stay across the street from the Consulate at the Hotel Playa Mazatlán—a grand resort in the center of Playa Gaviotas. The least the DEA could do, he said, in exchange for their help.

Now seated in a small meeting room at the Consulate, the group fielded various questions from Henderson and Wilson.

"Anna," Agent Henderson said. "You said your ex-husband …" He looked at his notepad. "Juan. You said he had something to do with this?"

"Yes, I think those men offered to pay him to find me. He just laughed when they took us."

"Got it. So, do you think he's involved with the cartel?"

"No. He's a simple fool. He wouldn't last a day with the cartel."

"Did you get everything you need from Aguado's

computer?" Reynolds cut in. "I mean, he smashed it into a million pieces."

Agent Wilson piped up. "Oh yeah, loads of stuff. We've got bank accounts, customers, distributors—you name it. The second he put that drive into his computer, we had access to everything. Didn't matter that he destroyed it after the fact."

"What happens to Aguado now?" Reynolds asked.

"He'll be extradited to the U.S. to face trial for his crimes against the American people. After that, he'll probably end up in Florence."

"Italy?" Reynolds asked, confused.

Henderson chuckled. "A little bit closer to home than that. Florence is a federal supermax prison in Colorado."

"Ah." Reynolds replied sheepishly.

"And what about the chemist, Felix Martin?" Anna asked.

"We had a good chat with him last night," Henderson replied. "He says he was kidnapped by the cartel and forced to create the formula. Said he owed them money, and they threatened to kill him if he didn't help them."

"Do you believe him?" Reynolds asked.

"We ran his name through the system and his background corroborates the timeline for his story. Plus, he's agreed to testify, which is huge since he has first-hand knowledge of Aguado's dealings."

"Don't you think the cartel will come after him?" Reynolds pressed.

"Hard to tell. But we'll stash him in a safe house anyway —somewhere we can protect him until the trial."

"What about us?" Danny asked.

"The amount of data we got from Aguado's network, coupled with Martin's testimony, should be enough to put him away for a long, long time. For now, I'm going to list the three of you as confidential informants and have your names redacted from any paperwork regarding the raid on Aguado's compound. It'll be like you were never there."

"I wish," Danny replied.

Henderson laughed and set down his pen on the yellow notepad in front of him. "Well, lady and gentlemen, unless you have more questions for us, I think we're done here. You can all go enjoy some well-earned vacation time."

The group stood and exchanged hugs and goodbyes with Henderson and Wilson. As they walked toward the exit, Henderson put a hand on Reynolds' shoulder. "If the gig at the Baseball Academy doesn't work out, give me a call. The DEA could use a good man like you."

"Remember when I told you I had a new perspective on life?" Reynolds asked. "Well, if this experience has taught me anything, it's that I belong in the Academy working with those kids. I think I found my purpose."

Henderson smiled. "Never hurts to ask."

As they left the building, Anna looked at Reynolds. "You want to spend some time on the beach today?"

"Sure do," Reynolds said. "I just need to run a quick errand first."

Anna eyed him suspiciously, then thought better of it. He was a grown man. He could do whatever he wanted. "Okay, we'll meet you back at the hotel later."

"Don't take too long," Danny said. "I'm going to school you in beach volleyball."

"You're on," Reynolds replied, and watched as Anna and Danny crossed the street between the Consulate and the hotel and disappeared inside the resort.

After a short wait, a green and white taxicab sped down the street in front of him and Reynolds waved a hand in the air. The driver slammed on the brakes, bringing the car to a screeching stop near the sidewalk where Reynolds stood.

"Adónde?" the driver asked.

"Academia de Béisbol de Sinaloa." Reynolds replied.

---

When he returned to the resort, Reynolds quickly found Anna and Danny and the trio spent the remainder of the day relaxing on the beach.

Reynolds and Danny took turns practicing their serves on the sand volleyball court and swam in the ocean while Anna lounged in the sun, sipping a large margarita and reading a book.

"Don't you two ever get tired?" she said, as Reynolds and Danny plopped down on the long folding beach chairs beside her.

"Can't let this guy get the better of me," Reynolds replied, pointing to Danny.

"Mom, why don't you come and play volleyball with us?" Danny asked.

"I've never really been on a vacation, Mijo. I just like sitting here in the sun."

Danny watched as two teenagers began hitting the ball back and forth on the volleyball court. "Let's go show these guys whose house this is, Dillon."

Reynolds glanced at Anna, who nodded tacitly and smiled back. "Go ahead."

"Alright." Reynolds replied. "One game and then we better go get ready for dinner."

"Dinner?" Anna asked.

"Yeah, I made us a reservation upstairs at Mariscos Playa. The lobster is supposed to be amazing." He flashed his trademark smile, and jogged to the volleyball court.

---

It turned out the lobster at Mariscos Playa wasn't the only thing that was amazing. The patio provided a breathtaking view of the ocean and the setting sun as it dipped below the horizon, wrapped in ribbons of orange and crimson.

The group ordered drinks and recounted the harrowing events they'd endured over the previous few days. The discussion eventually turned to how lucky they'd all been to have escaped relatively unscathed. All except for Reynolds, who was deemed to have a mild concussion. But the doctor had told him the prescription for that was rest—and there was plenty of that to be had here at the resort.

As they chatted, Reynolds reached into the backpack he'd casually brought into the restaurant and pulled out a large, plain manilla envelope.

Danny's eyes narrowed, and Anna turned to look at Reynolds. "And what do you have there?" she said coyly.

"Well, I remembered we have some unfinished business from the other night. So, I ran over to the Academy and got copies of Danny's offers." He held up the envelope casually. "Anyone want to take a look?"

Danny beamed from across the table. "Dillon, I thought you forgot."

"Nah, besides, a little bird told me the Twins put a whole bunch of zeros in their offer. I wanted to be here when you saw it. Now, how about you open this before something else crazy happens?"

The group shared a laugh as Reynolds handed Danny the envelope and he quickly tore it open. One-by-one he went through the offers, studying each word. Reynolds was impressed. Danny didn't just skip to the part that contained the signing bonus. He pored through the verbiage on each document, deciphering some parts himself and asking for help on others.

When he'd read through each offer letter in its entirety,

he laid them in three separate piles on the table. "I choose this one," he said, and picked up the offer from the Minnesota Twins.

Reynolds inwardly cheered Danny's decision. Not only was their offer higher than that of the Astros or the Reds, but his conversations with the Twins' scout, James Duncan, had reassured him the organization was the right fit for Danny.

Danny handed the Twins' offer to Anna and watched as his mother skimmed the contract. Reynolds waited patiently for her reaction. He wanted to see her face when reached the dollar figure.

But instead of a smile or a gasp or even a scream, tears began to stream down her face. She tried to wipe them away, but the moment was too great. All her hopes and dreams for Danny were suddenly coming true. The hard work. The sacrifice. The bond they had formed over his short fourteen years. Now he had a chance to leave Villa Unión. A chance to create a better life.

"What's wrong, Mom?" Danny asked. "Do you want me to choose one of the other offers?"

She laughed and dabbed at her eyes with the corner of a napkin. "No, Mijo. These are tears of joy. I'm so proud of you."

Anna reached across the table and squeezed his hand. "But listen, Mr. Big Shot. You can't forget about your mother when you're rich and famous." She eyed Danny seriously. "Promise?"

"I promise, Mom," Danny replied, smile widening.

Reynolds watched Anna and Danny, not wanting to interrupt the moment. He too, was proud of Danny. But not just Danny. He was proud of Anna, as well. She'd handled a terrifying situation with uncommon grit and determination. She was an amazing woman.

As he watched, a team of waiters arrived at the table with steaming plates of New England lobster, cups of lemon and garlic butter, and large wooden bowls of salad. It was a dinner that had been a long time in the making.

Before they could dig in, Anna cleared her throat. "Dillon, I just wanted to say thank you for everything. Not just for coming to our rescue, but for being such a good man. You are truly a hero."

"Yeah, thanks Dillon," Danny cut in. "You're a good friend."

Reynolds stared back, first at Danny, then at Anna. "You're both pretty cool too." He flashed his trademark smile and gestured around the table at the extravagant spread. "Welcome to the big leagues."

Printed in Great Britain
by Amazon